2,000 VOICES

Young Adolescents' Perceptions and Curriculum Implications

National Middle School Association is dedicated to improving the educational experiences of young adolescents by providing vision, knowledge, and resources to all who serve them in order to develop healthy, productive, and ethical citizens.

2,000 VOICES

Young Adolescents' Perceptions and Curriculum Implications

by
Cynthia S. Mee

National Middle School Association
Columbus, Ohio

National Middle School Association
2600 Corporate Exchange Drive, Suite 370
Columbus, Ohio 43231
Telephone (800) 528-NMSA

Printed in the United States of America

Sue Swaim, Executive Director
Jeff Ward, Director of Business Services
John Lounsbury, Editor
Mary Mitchell, Copy Editor/Designer
Marcia Meade, Publications Sales

LB
1623.5
.M44
1997
apu.1999

ISBN: 1-56090-116-0   NMSA Stock Number: 1242

Library of Congress Cataloging-in-Publication Data

Mee, Cynthia S., date-
    2,000 voices: young adolescents' perceptions and curriculum implications/Cynthia S. Mee.
      p. cm.
    Includes bibliographical references (p.).
    ISBN 1-56090-116-0 (pbk.)
    1. Middle school students--United States--Psychology.
2. Adolescent psychology--United States. 3. Curriculum planning--United States.   I. Title
LB1623.5.M44 1997
373.18'01'9--dc21
                                    97-5315
                                      CIP

Dedication

... to Don Eichhorn and John Lounsbury who have been and are visionaries for young adolescents and whose dedication to young adolescents we should all emulate. Thanks, Don and John.

This volume is also dedicated to OmniObadiah Kirkjohnathan Mee who at just seven years of age modeled the independence of thought that children have and challenged me with this research idea one night when we were eating pizza. He also traveled with me to the school sites, missed out on other pizza dinners, and supported me at the computer hour after hour so I could complete the writing of this project. My only wish is that all parents could be so fortunate as to have such a supportive child.

Acknowledgements

Abundant thanks to the students in my Characteristics of the Transescent class, summer 1993, at the University of Wisconsin-Platteville, for their assistance in analyzing the data. Thanks also goes to Carol Flores for help in editing the manuscript, to Wendy Kelly, Stacy Schneider, and Joan Neilson for typing the student data and contributing to the analyses of what the young adolescents wrote. I also want to express genuine appreciation to all the principals and schools who let me come into their schools (Tenaya Middle and Sadler Elementary Schools in Fresno, California; Sierra Elementary School, Sierra, California; Menlo Park Middle School, Menlo Park, California; Westridge and Walker Middle Schools, and Baird and Lancaster Elementary Schools in Orlando, Florida; Talawanda Middle School, Oxford, Ohio; St. Mary's and Platteville Middle Schools, Platteville, Wisconsin; Galena Middle School, Galena, Illinois; and P.S. 87 and I.S. 44 Schools, New York City).

Jim King, who regularly came to my rescue at the computer, saved my damaged disks, and kept me from going crazy because of my computer illiteracy deserves a word of appreciation.

A final and very special expression of gratitude goes to the 2,000 young adolescents who shared their thoughts first with me and now with the readers. You are the book. I hope the book represents you well. Thanks.

Contents

About the Author

Cynthia S. Mee is a professor of education at National-Louis University, Evanston, Illinois. A former teacher in diverse cultures in all grade levels, pre-K through college, Dr. Mee is an active leader in professional associations and in efforts to advance the middle school movement. Her particular areas of interest are early adolescent development, gender issues, and the media impact on gender identification of young adolescents.

Foreword

2,000 Voices is a photograph in time of the young adolescent's culture. When we add the voices to the picture we obtain a script that should be required reading for everyone who touches the lives of 10-15 year old students. The questions asked guide the respondents through a self-portrait of such immense importance to teachers that it cannot be ignored. There is good news in these voices. They form a chorale of hope and affirmation that the world about us is not as bad as we are sometimes led to believe. Cynthia Mee has done what many of us in education have wanted to do – she heard the voices, recorded the song, and painted the picture bringing us a vivid glimpse into a time that is today in our children's lives and yesterday in our lives. Questions such as "What hasn't happened in your life you would like to happen…" and "Power is …" delve deep into the hearts and minds of the 2,000 students who participated. Their responses are candid, painfully honest, surprisingly hopeful, while speculative about their place in the future.

The gender differences emphasized by the responses to multiple questions make a significant contribution to the current research on gender. For this group as well as many others who have been interviewed, it appears that the best thing about being a boy is not being a girl — and the best things about being a girl are hair and being pretty.

This book is the result of a forum of opportunities offered to students who might not otherwise have had an opportunity to express themselves. Teachers can use this book to increase their own understanding, to stimulate dialog with their students, to encourage their hearing, and to make curriculum and instruction changes based on the voices of students.

— Sherrel Bergmann

Emperor:	*Now we will go to school.*
Mr. Johnston:	*Your Majesty, in my country it is usual to begin with some kind of an examination.*
Emperor:	*The Emperor cannot be examined.*
Mr. Johnston:	*Now that may have to change. But first Your Majesty might like to ask me some questions.*
Emperor:	*Where are your ancestors buried?*
Mr. Johnston:	*In Scotland, Your Majesty.*
Emperor:	*But then where's your skirt? In your country men wear short skirts, do they not?*
Mr. Johnston:	*No, Your Majesty, Scotsmen do not wear skirts, they wear kilts.*
Emperor:	*Kilts?*
Mr. Johnston:	*Kilts. A matter of words, perhaps, but words are important.*
Emperor:	*Why are words important?*
Mr. Johnston:	*If you can't say what you mean, Your Majesty, you will never mean what you say; and a gentleman should always mean what he says.*
Emperor:	*Ah, yes, a gentleman. Are you a gentleman?*
Mr. Johnston:	*I would like to be a gentleman, Your Majesty. I try to be.*
Emperor:	*I am not a gentleman. I am not allowed to say what I mean. They are always telling me what to say.*
Mr. Johnston:	*Your Majesty is still very young.*

— Movie, *The Last Emperor*

1.
Young Adolescents and Their Social Realities

Young adolescents are more than simply that portion of the population going through puberty. They comprise a particularly critical group as they travel from childhood to adolescence and then into young adulthood, making decisions that determine the nature of their futures. In this transition these 10-14 year-olds are exposed daily to thousands of adult messages. They live and interact in the adult world of media, war, divorce, gangs, work, HIV virus, drugs, alcohol, and violence – all this while simultaneously going through the most extensive developmental changes in the human life cycle.

To better appreciate and understand young adolescents middle level educators often rely on a PIES theory of development (**physical, intellectual, emotional,** and **social**), and recognize that as one matures such changes occur sporadically and seldom in harmony. But at the same time the PIES theory needs to be more inclusive and embrace the realities of society, including one's moral development and memberships in one's gender, socioeconomic, spiritual, and cultural group. The impact these aspects have on developmental characteristics to PIES contribute to a theory I call PIES PLUS. As we work with the PIES PLUS theory educators need to examine the close link that exists between emotional and social aspects. A shift from the current S (social) to a spiritual S might be a consideration for a change. Many students have a religious affiliation, or more broadly speaking, a spiritual side to their lives. For example, how students choose to worship, treat their bodies and the earth, and the processes they choose when making decisions in daily practice may reflect that spiritual dimension. Educators can appreciate, without bias, this spiritual connection to how young adolescents grow and develop.

All elements of society contribute to what young adolescents think, value, know, and believe. Since no two individuals experience life the same, young adolescents cannot view the world or the world of school identically. Teachers know that all students do not learn identically and that it is important to know more about them and the social realities under which they live. To understand them fully, educators should go directly to students and learn how they view the world, school, and their own learning.

To understand students, educators should go directly to them and learn how they view the world, school, and their own learning.

Why Examine Middle School Voices?

This book presents the thoughts young adolescents have about themselves and their world, primarily in their own words. The young adolescents have painted the world in which they live and learn. Their thoughts vary, and the way they use words may be different from one another and from the adult world where they live and are educated. It is not a new journey to explore the young adolescent culture. As early as 1948 child developmentalist Robert J. Havighurst expressed the need to understand the social realities of learners:

> Nature lays down the wide possibilities in the developing of the human body, and which possibilities shall be realized depends on what the individual learns. This is true even of such crude biological realities of feeding habits and sexual relations, while the more highly social realities of language, economic behavior, and religion are almost completely the product of learning at the hands of society. (1972, pp.1-2)

Such a recognition of young adolescent development, learning, language, culture, and thought is the motivation behind this study.

The thoughts were secured in what might be termed a quasi-ethnographic study. In *Looking at Lives Through Ethnography* Margaret Finders (1992) cites Brodkey's description of ethnography as a richly textured description of community life that allows us to understand others on their terms.

To understand young adolescents, I went to 15 schools in six states and recorded the reflections of the young adolescents enrolled there. A more comprehensive look into the thoughts of students would have been to go to their environments outside of school, their homes, the malls, and their hangouts. These environments show a "way with words" as described by Shirley Heath (1983) that is distinctly theirs. While within the school setting students are often expected to conform to a certain degree in thought and behavior. When I visited the schools I tried to discourage students from thinking they had to conform to any thoughts but their own.

Young adolescents live in a dynamic society. These frequent changes make it difficult for adults to keep pace and make appropriate adaptations to the conditions in society. Adults believe they know what and how young adolescents think because they were young once. But the social context and realities that they knew growing up are not the same as those experienced by young adolescents today. This gap between age groups inevitably separates them. Yet it is through the historic perspective of adults that the education of youth is determined.

Adults believe they know what and how young adolescents think because they were young once. But the social context and realities that they knew growing up are not the same as those today.

What I Wanted to Learn

While growing up I kept waiting to learn what I thought important or what I wanted to learn. I remember suggesting my ideas to various teachers along the way. They would tell me, in effect, that's a nice idea but it's not part of the curriculum or it doesn't fit into what we are studying. I always wondered what curriculum was; no one defined or described it. It was a big secret to me.

After awhile I gave up suggesting ideas and started to play the "education game." I didn't stop having ideas, I just stopped suggesting them to teachers. I used my own ideas for awhile until I realized that the students who used the teachers' ideas received better grades and earned greater approval from the educational establishment than I did.

I discovered that the ideas teachers liked were "traditional" or ones that the teachers agreed with or knew. In my own very young mind I figured out there was no connection between what I cared about and what the school valued. The resulting attitude took away much of the fun and involvement of learning for me. I attended a laboratory school; we had coed industrial arts and home economics; we had a CORE curriculum and did not get grades on report cards; we had physical education every day, and music and art at least three times a week; anyone who wanted to be on a team was on the team, and anyone who wanted to be a cheerleader was one. My 1950s junior high school education was quite similar to what is advocated in middle level education today. I was luckier than most. But one thing was missing, we did not have a curriculum connected to our social realities and our interests.

I continued to play the education game throughout my junior high, high school, and college years, and kept hoping with each level of education for a connection with my interests. Some theorists might say this was an egocentric thought, but all I knew was that something was missing in my education. I learned to stop thinking, and worse, I stopped constructing knowledge, a phenomena experienced by many young adolescents (Belenky, 1986; Brown, 1990; Gilligan, 1992; Sadker & Sadker, 1993).

This curriculum control even occurred in graduate school. I was discouraged from taking classes and doing research focusing on my interests. I needed to take those required classes. I'll never forget the first day I met with my advisor and was enthusiastically bursting forth with my ideas. He said, "I have other plans for you." And before I knew it, I was doing his plan. After all "he knew what was important for me."

I survived the schooling process, but many students who felt as I did dropped out of school or just hung in there long enough to graduate. Such students are still being lost today because their ideas are not taken seriously or because the interests they have and bring to school are not connected to the school curriculum already in place.

Students are being lost today because the interests they have and
bring to school are not connected to
the schooling process.

I constantly think of the wasted talent and minds lost because students lose interest in education, their education. We
must stop losing the potential of youth and make formal education a vital learning experience connected to the realities of their
lives. Today teachers are trying harder than ever to address student needs, but many still do it from the teacher's knowledge
and experience base, functioning from their own social realities. At a time when schools are losing students at an alarming
rate, it is essential that educators look seriously at the differences between the social realities of the teachers and those of
the students and be willing to make needed adjustments in perceptions and in the way they conduct schooling.

During the middle
school years young
adolescents begin to
make lifelong deci-
sions concerning their
futures.

Since it is during the middle school years that young adolescents begin to make lifelong decisions concerning their futures
(AAUW, 1992; NMSA, 1995), it is important for teachers to study
them and their culture closely. When educators understand fully
young adolescent realities, student learning will become more
meaningful, and the lifelong decisions they formulate will be
more positive.

This study is based on the premise that if we as educators
know what is important to students and understand their social realities, then maybe we can relate and connect these students' attitudes, thought, and values to the schooling process.
When this occurs, education will become the exciting, safe, eq-
uitable, and authentic experience it ought to be. School will be
a place where students want to attend and where their positive
energy and passion are engaged in meaningful ways.

What a Child Taught Me

A second source of motivation behind this study was introduced to me by a seven-year-old child. I was getting ready to teach a class on a day that he didn't have school. He casually said, "If I were to teach your class you know what I would do?" I replied, "No, what would you do?" I wish I could remember his exact words, but I remember the special nature of his response, and as a result I invited him to be a guest speaker. He accepted my offer and taught one of the most charming classes I have ever observed. I could not have been more surprised or pleased with how he spoke to the class. The first question from one of my students was "What is the most important quality a teacher can have?" He thought about it for a moment and then responded "Getting homework back in a timely fashion." Is this the kind of answer you would have expected from a second grader? Not me. I was surprised.

His answers continued on this level. He presented his perceptions to the class, most of which were totally unexpected. I thought I knew my child well and could anticipate his responses. On this day I learned that this young child had thoughts of his own. He owned his knowledge and presented it in a fashion that I learned to respect, understand, and encourage. I also realized that if one child can have such intense thoughts, then other children must also.

The enthusiasm I experienced was shared by my class. My college students were awed by this seven-year-old's behavior and thinking. From that time on, I always try to include children in my class curricula. I want my students to experience children's perceptions of society, and come to know that children of all ages think and have ownership of their thoughts.

Language and Thought

A third motivation for this research came from the notion that knowledge is usually expressed through language, verbal or nonverbal, and that language names our experiences and defines our world. Language is built on one's perceptions and has the ability to shape or silence people. How well one uses language in school can determine one's success in school. The same is true in life. Therefore, educators must ask in whose language, whose ideas, and whose curricula do schools structure the learning process?

Sociolinguists indicate that language is a special code needed to be mastered as well as voiced in order for individuals to fit into society and transform information into knowledge. The cultural code created through language has the power to discriminate in the curriculum taught (ability grouping) and the curriculum understood (interpreted and evaluated).

Most subject content is presented in the language of a cultural code established by certain socioeconomic classes. Individuals who live outside the established code might be excluded from the learning process because their past experiences have not provided the needed foundation. Because of this lack of "proper" language some students may feel uncomfortable in the classroom, more like "outsiders." This may lead to being diagnosed as learning disabled and then placed in a different educational setting. If education is inclusive of students' thoughts and a greater use of student language, then the educational process might become more comfortable and significant for young adolescents.

Voices and Curriculum

The concept of making the curriculum relate to children's knowledge and experiences is not new. In the early 20th century Dewey (1938) suggested that subject matter should not be hard and fast nor fixed outside the child's experience; it should be viewed as fluent, vital, embryonic. Beane and Lipka (1987) believe learning doesn't just happen in the classroom and that the success of young adolescents' learning is enhanced through the development of a strong self-esteem. They support the notion that during this process a young adolescent changes from a child's self-view of "I am what I do" to "I am who I am." They suggest that educators need to remember how and where learning occurs:

> Curriculum consists of all the experiences of the learner
> under the auspices of the school. Learning is not confined
> to the classroom nor is it limited to the intentions described
> in the curriculum documents such as course syllabi. Young
> people learn in the hallways, on buses, on playgrounds,

and in the principal's office. They learn from expectations
of teachers, from interactions with peers, and from ways
in which they are treated as people and as students. It is
in these settings and by these means that young people
come to know something of themselves and their relation-
ships to others. This is the hidden curriculum. What is
learned here is more powerful than the lessons of the in-
tended curriculum plans since this is the part which
touches, most deeply, the self-perceptions, values, and
attitudes of learners. (p.17)

This broader recognition of the learning environment is important since it has tremendous influence on the development of young adolescents. The total school environment contributes to the social realities of students. It provides the places in which young adolescents attempt to make sense of their world and develop their social relationships. A letter I received from Peggy (1995), a 6th grade student, that was designed to tell me a little about herself and her schooling experience describes her social realities:

Dear Dr. Mee:

Some things I think you should know about me are:
#1 my name does not fit me, "The girl next door" definitely isn't me, so I think I give my own meaning to the word Peggy. Number two, I love dogs, and not just like the average person. I love dogs like most people love their siblings (without the fighting). I have three dogs. Number four, I am in the middle of everything at school. To explain this I have to tell you about the groups in school. The first group is the ultra cool group which consists of Shira, Brook, and Karen and sometimes Jess, sometimes Todd and sometimes Nick and Bridgett. The second group is Cindy, Kathleen (best friends), Sarah, Becky, Thia, and sometimes me. Then there's the guys group (most of the guys are in it). There is also what we call "the pink ladies." This group includes Paula, Leslie, Jane, Lory, Katie, Matt, Darrell, Shelly, Liz and Jenny. Now that you know who's in what group you'll know I'm not really in any of them. I guess I kind of commute from one to another. The boys treat me like I was a boy and don't mind talking about what "girls they like" around me. Some-

times Brook and Shira will let me in with them. The main group I hang out with now is Cindy, Kathleen, etc. I never hang out with the pink ladies, and that is about it.

Peggy

This letter from Peggy demonstrates her view of school and the hidden curriculum that contributes to the classroom atmosphere.

The total school environment provides the places in which young adolescents attempt to make sense of their world and develop their social relationships.

In school students have many opportunities to develop certain behaviors of acceptance and approval, or experience the fears of rejection and isolation. Once students accept who they are and become comfortable with themselves they learn to like themselves. Unfortunately, many students going through this transition have difficulty learning to like themselves. According to the AAUW's 1992 study *How Schools Shortchange Girls*, students experience a decline in self-esteem during the middle school years which for boys levels off but for girls continues throughout high school. When educators understand the social realities of young adolescents they can assist students in completing the transition more gracefully and help them to develop more positive self-esteem.

As you read the many and varied perceptions of young adolescents provided in this study, think in terms of how their ideas might be connected to your class and its curricula. Through their responses in Chapter 2 young adolescents have defined their world and culture in their own words. Chapter 3 categorizes the students' voices into generalizations, and Chapter 4 provides curricula implications from the identified trends.

Beane (1993) addresses a need for educators to direct what they know about young adolescent development and curriculum content toward making needed curriculum change. He writes:

The importance of the fundamental but bypassed "curriculum question" cannot be overestimated since it opens the way to several key issues that supposedly guide the middle school movement but are only partially addressed by organizational reform. For example, if early adolescence is a distinct stage in human development and if middle school is to be based on the characteristics of that stage, then presumably the curriculum would be designed along developmental lines and would thus look different from that at other levels. If "reform" means that the relationships between schools, including teachers, and early adolescents are to be reconstructed, then the curriculum, as one of the powerful mediating forces in that relationship, would be presumably changed. (p.6)

Most educators would agree that the better teachers know their students the better they can teach them. If middle schools exist to address the developmental needs of young adolescents then the next step is to discover the uniqueness of those students in your school and create curricula that embraces what is vital to those students. One of the best ways of knowing students is to discover their social realities. What young adolescents indicated in their responses in this research project is what John Lounsbury has said for years; young adolescents are persons first, then students. This belief will become even more apparent as you study the social realities of the young adolescents you teach.

Educators agree that the better teachers know their students the better they can teach them....One of the best ways of knowing students is to discover their social realities.

Collecting Student Voices

To hear student voices I interviewed young adolescents in almost 100 classes, and collected their responses from 53 open-ended statements. 2,000 students in grades five through eight were involved. I walked them through the instrument (Appendix A). I used the term "statementaire" because the students wrote their responses to open-ended statement stems rather than responding to questions (Appendix B). I created most of them, but several were contributed by students who participated in the pilot study.

With an open-ended statementaire rather than a questionnaire I thought their responses might be freed from the test mentality. With a questionnaire format students might be more likely to provide answers they thought I wanted rather than what they actually thought.

The students genuinely seemed to enjoy being involved in the study. It was evident by their eagerness to ask questions and how they readily wrote their responses. They appreciated the challenge and the opportunity to be involved. As they finished, they would thank me for coming, for the experience, and some asked me to come back and do it again. I consider these as indicators of appreciation that someone cared about them and what they thought.

When I work in the schools I go by "Dr. Mee." I do this not out of personal ego but primarily to represent a role model to the students so that they may think they could have a doctor attached to their names. I also use the title to help justify my being there.

Prior to asking the students to write their responses I engage them in an informal dialogue. In this discussion I ask the students what are different types of doctors they go to or know. Their responses ranged from the expected variety of medical doctors, to veterinarians, and psychologists. When I called on a student I would ask for his/her last name and then put that name on the board with "Dr." before it. This technique allowed the students to think of themselves as persons who might become doctors or professionals. Their body language changed when I called them doctor during the remander of my time with them. After one of the classes a teacher said to me, "I could not believe it when you called ____ doctor. It was difficult for me to keep a straight face, he is such a poor student, but it made me think that it is possible he might become a doctor."

Eventually, I explained to the students that I spend a lot of time studying education and young people and ways of making education more exciting for them. I explained that I came to their school in order to get their thoughts and ideas and then to share them with other educators. They liked this challenge and graciously volunteered to participate. During this dialogue I sought to gain the trust of the students, thereby ensuring the validity of the research data.

Data Analysis

I initially thought that all I would have to do was tabulate the responses from the statementaires and that the consensus views of young adolescents would be obvious. Simply compiling the students' thoughts was a difficult task. The number of responses, both in the similarity and the diversity, and the range of them from funny to sad, made it difficult to organize them. I quickly realized that the social realities of these young adolescents were not what most adults probably assumed, and I wanted to provide an accurate and honest account of the students' responses so their culture could be reflected in a meaningful way.

Gender - The thoughts of young adolescents were clearly defined along gender lines. Although this study was not initially focused on gender, the findings emphatically indicated that the greatest differences in responses were gender based. This should not be surprising in light of recent gender studies (AAUW, 1991, 1992, 1993, 1995; Belenky and associates, 1986; Carlip, 1995; Gilligan, 1982; Gilligan, Lyons & Hammer, 1990; Gilligan & Mickel-Brown, 1992; Orenstein, 1994; Pipher, 1994; Riley, Baldus, Belson, Schuler, & Keyes, 1993). I particularly encourage readers to be sensitive to gender characteristics and the developmental differences between young adolescent girls and boys as they work with students.

The thoughts of young adolescents were clearly defined along gender lines....Geographic and cultural diversity factors were not as apparent as gender differences.

Diversity - At the top of the statementaire there was a place for identification of age, gender, brothers and sisters and their ages, and an ethnic breakdown as defined by the Wisconsin Department of Public Instruction (DPI). The ethnic categories were not comprehensive enough; other populations needed to be included as well as a "mixed" category. Grade, age, and gender were used for basic breakdown of the responses. After the pilot study I asked for information about brothers, sisters, and their ages. Many responses in the first several groups of students I compiled frequently mentioned getting "beat up" a lot. I thought about it and realized that many of the responses had to do with older and/or younger brothers and sisters, and that was part of the negative aspects of their age group.

Geographic and cultural diversity factors were not quite as apparent as gender differences. However, students from New York, California, and Florida appeared to be more globally aware and concerned about poverty, the homeless population, and the environment than students in the Midwest. Much young adolescent male humor tended to be sexist and racist, and this, too was more apparent in the Midwest. When a racist joke was told on the coasts, students usually apologized. It was more common for boys to tell both racist and/or sexist jokes. Silly jokes were very common from all populations, especially "knock-knock" and "why the chicken crossed the road" types of jokes.

Young adolescents living on the coasts and from diverse cultures had a greater variety of food choices, but pizza was the all-time favorite food of young adolescents.

Reading and Analyzing Student Thoughts

As you read the responses in this study, there are various theories important to remember. Four that I encourage you to recall are: Maslow's hierarchy of needs (1970), Piaget's cognitive developmental stages (1952), Gilligan's (1982, 1990, 1992) moral reasoning development, and Havighurst's (1972) developmental tasks.

Maslow's hierarchy of needs sets forth the notion that the first needs to satisfy are physiological (food and drink) followed by psychological (safety, love, and esteem) and that each need can be met only after the preceding one has been satisfied. The highest order of needs Maslow suggests are metaneeds (aesthetic, cognitive, and self-actualization). The high level of self-actualization stimulates our desire to develop an aesthetic appreciation of beauty, truth, and knowledge and to continue to grow and become fulfilled. Maslow's first two stages are of particular interest for middle school students.

Educators should ask themselves basic questions about student needs. How can students learn if they do not feel safe? How can students learn if restroom policies do not accommodate the needs of changing young bodies? How can students learn if they are hungry? How can students learn if they are being yelled at, embarrassed, or made fun of by parents, siblings, friends, teachers, or administrators? Is it reasonable under such circumstances to assume that they will possess enough self-esteem to commit their energies to learning? The likelihood of learning decreases markedly when these more basic needs are not being satisfied.

Piaget established developmentally based cognitive stages. His first two stages, sensorimotor (birth-age 2) and preoperational stage (ages 2-7), are for the most part completed by the time students reach fifth grade. Most young adolescents are at the operational stage during much of middle school; however, progress into the formal operational stage is evident by the time they reach eighth grade. It is apparent through the responses of the students in this study that most fifth and sixth graders were still at the concrete operational level. Eighth grade responses, on the other hand, indicated that many of them were beginning to enter the formal operational levels, especially the girls. Many student responses fell somewhere between these two levels. With this in mind, it is obvious that some content and some instructional strategies may not be effective for some students but will be for others.

During middle school years young adolescents are regularly faced with making major moral decisions.

During the middle school years young adolescents are faced with making major moral decisions. It is important to understand that there are not only different stages of moral development (Kohlberg 1976, 1984) but also different approaches. Gilligan (1982) states that women view moral dilemmas and questions differently than men. She contends that women's decisions tend to be influenced by interpersonal relationships and the needs of others more than men, and that as men approach moral reasoning they are predisposed more in a legalistic and individualistic manner.

During early adolescence girls and boys approach adulthood differently. Boys are taught to be autonomous while girls are encouraged to develop relationships, attachments, and connections to others. Gilligan and Mikel-Brown (1992) further highlight this gender difference of young adolescents. Girls have been raised to value relationships and to define themselves through their relationships with others. As they begin to think and act on their individual interests, goals, and needs to become self-sufficient they are faced with a challenge they do not know is coming and do not really understand. A conflict occurs as they attempt to become autonomous while trying to stay connected and maintain inclusionary relationships.

As girls try on different ideas and identities they get labeled and targeted by others. Teachers can see this conflict frequently throughout the middle school years. They know how abusive some girls can be to other girls. This is often because on the road to adulthood girls are trying to blend two worlds, two worlds that no one warned them about. It can be a painful process.

The problem then becomes how can teachers and parents best provide girls the opportunities to be individuals yet comfortably stay connected to their friends and family? Throughout this research project girls indicated this struggle and their need for a caring supportive environment.

Young adolescents are very much in a transitional state, not quite a child, yet not quite a teenager. Their emotions are on the surface as they try to make sense of the world in which they live. Havighurst (1972) identified various developmental tasks that young adolescents face including physical maturation, cultural pressures of society, and personal values and aspirations. He especially recognized the value of understanding this sensitive period and cited how psychologists viewed this developmental stage:

In their respective ways, von Senden, Lorenz, Sptiz, and Piaget have observed phenomena which suggest that there may be critical periods in the development of the child – points or stages during which the organism is maximally receptive to specific stimuli. Such stages may exist in the development of fundamental sensory processes, such as conceptions about size, shape, and distance, and in the development of social behavior as well. The critical periods hypothesize that these stages are of limited duration: there may be a finite period during which certain experiences must occur if they are to become part of the organism's repertoire of responses; or there may be a period of increased efficiency for the acquisition of experience, before which it cannot be assimilated and after which the level of receptivity remains constant. (p. 6)

As you read the responses of these young adolescents try to see the world through their eyes, minds, and bodies and relate them to young adolescent development theory. It may have been a long time since you were a young adolescent, but try to recall what it was like.

It is up to educators to remember this sensitive but vaguely defined period and how challenging it is for young adolescents. Educators need to listen to young adolescents if they are to guide them in their development and keep the level of receptivity of experiences open, fluid, and relevant. The payoff will be confident young adolescents making the transition from the stage of "I am what I do" to the "I am who I am" stage while working positively toward self-actualization. **v**

2.

Young Adolescent Responses in Summary

While there was an interesting variety in the responses of these fifth, sixth, seventh, and eighth graders to the items on the statementaire, common threads were readily apparent. The frequency of certain responses, the most commonly given answers, open doors to educators anxious to truly understand and enter the world of young adolescents. Brief summaries of the students' responses to all 53 questions comprise this chapter, while the next chapter offers analyses of these typical perceptions. Students actual words are italicized.

1. Truth is... Most responses represented the basic responses for all grades, cultures, and both genders: *being honest, not lying, correct answers, telling what really happened.*

2. Knowledge is... Young adolescents found it difficult to articulate their thoughts on knowledge but generally said: *smarts; knowing something; education; someone old and wise;* and *knowing what you are supposed to know.*

3. Power is... *Mom, teachers, God, Jesus, parents* were common responses. Sometimes very concrete responses were *electricity* and *muscles.* Fifth and sixth grade boys typically saw power as something physical, like strength. Some younger girls and boys saw power as somebody or something while seventh and eighth grade students viewed peer groups, popularity, and cliques as types of power.

4. Who controls?... *The oldest person of a group, God, Jesus, parents, teachers,* and *principals* were common responses. Eighth grade students often stated that money and government have control. While boys saw control in terms of national leaders, girls looked to control from parents, teachers, and principals. No women or minority other than mothers and teachers were mentioned as having power. Generally young adolescents saw power and control as being closely related.

5. Rules are... *To keep us safe; things to be obeyed; laws; not to be broken; boring,* and *guidelines.* Safety was viewed as an aspect of rules, to prevent chaos and to provide order. Some eighth graders did think that rules were made to be broken.

6. It is important to know... *Who your friends are; about disease; history; math,* and *reading; the school dress code; who to trust; safe sex; not to take drugs; about life; know your manners; how to protect your reputation; right from wrong; don't walk in alleys; how we are more fortunate than others;* and *how to say 'no.'*
Boys more than girls mentioned school and academics as important to know: *math; how to read; what you want in the future; how to learn; your decision on something; school subjects;* and *how to change your grade on a grade card.* Girls rarely mentioned academics as important to know and saw survival skills as valued to know: *safe sex; stay out of alleys; who your friends are; how to stay 'no;' the truth.* Girls thought of survival first; they appear to have learned at a young age they need to know what to do rather than how to use knowledge. On the other hand, boys have learned that knowledge is needed to survive.

7. I would like to tell my friends... The advice given to their friends included: *hoping their friends would be nicer; to stop teas-*

Power is...   Rules are...

ing; to stop picking on me and others; and *to stop being cruel to others.* An opposite view was represented by saying that they loved their friends and thanked them for the support: *thanks for being there; that I do trust them; secrets;* and *things that have happened to me.* Many of the responses were sad, because so many young adolescents thought their friends teased them or made fun of them or that some young adolescents had problems at home that they wanted to share but couldn't. Friends were viewed as important to young adolescents to share their secrets with and to hang out with. Girls' friendships involved a lot of talking to each other and demonstrated more communication and moral support. Boys' friendships were autonomous, open, free-flowing relationships that did not focus on communication rather on doing things, having fun, and sticking up for each other.

8. I would like to tell my family... Young adolescents wanted to get advice and support from parents, share their thoughts and concerns, and spend time and experiences with them. Common responses included: *I love them; how I feel; what I am doing in school; stop picking on me; stop yelling; let's do more things together; leave me alone; stay out of my room; give me privacy; everything;* and *thanks for being there.* The responses to this statement indicated that young adolescents were young enough to want parental love and nurturing but old enough to want and need privacy. Most of the advice to parents was positive. Sometimes young adolescents asked for material things or wanted to move, while some advised their parents to stop fighting and to try to get along. For the most part a positive family trend was apparent in the responses. However, it was obvious that some young adolescents face problems at home and have little or no control over them.

9. I would like to advise my teachers... Young adolescents wanted their teachers to: *lighten up, teach so we can have fun; have a sense of humor; be more caring, have less homework;*

I would like to tell my family...

have more projects; teach so I can understand; stop being mean; they are special to me; stop yelling; stop having favorites; and *thanks for being there.* The responses were amazingly similar at all grade levels. When observing differences between genders the advice the boys gave was more task oriented on how to teach, while advice given by girls was focused on how to be more caring and supportive. Both genders saw a need for more communication and openness with teachers, less homework, more humor, and advice for teachers to: *lighten up, get a life,* and *to get better substitutes.*

10. I would like to advise my principal... Common advice and comments were: *tell teachers to be happier and to be less strict and more interesting; be more understanding of kids; give kids more choices; shorten the school day; have fewer days of school; more recesses; don't be sexist; more field trips; have better chairs; check on the teachers more often; get better substitute teachers;* and that *he/she is doing a good job.* Personal advice consisted of: *lose weight; stop smoking; keep being funny,* and *don't be mean and bossy.* Both genders and students from all geographic regions felt that principals need to be more aware and understanding of situations and that they need to be fair and consistent when decisions are made. At the same time they thought principals should mind their own business. Girls tended to regard principals as being more friendly and nice, while the boys portend to be more afraid of principals. Young adolescents in schools with women principals perceived their principals as more caring and supportive than students at schools with male principals. Young adolescents with male principals saw them as authoritarian, less personable, and less approachable than did students at schools with women principals.

11. I am happy when... *being treated nice; treating others nice;* and *being with family first and then friends.* Other responses included when: *people make me feel good; I'm having fun; getting good grades; doing things with the family; I have done a*

I am happy when...

good deed; hanging out with friends; school is out; parents or teachers do or say something nice; and I don't have any homework. The seventh and eighth graders mentioned their friends more frequently than younger middle school students. Almost no one stated that getting things made him/her happy.

12. A goal I have in life is to... The stated goals of most of the young adolescents were wanting to: be a pro-athlete; travel, especially out of the country or out of state; have a family; make people nicer to each other; and get a college education. By seventh and eighth grade boys appeared to have more specific goals than girls. The goals that girls had tended to be more generalized and romantic. When boys mentioned having a family they were more specific in what they wanted their wives to be like, and the number of children. Girls wanted: to be a good wife; to be mother; to have a good career; and to be the best person they can be. Boys also mentioned joining the armed forces as a goal. Only a few girls mentioned the military as an option. Boys clearly have more specific goals than girls. If girls do have goals, they are not as clearly defined as those of the boys.

13. My favorite life experience is... I was surprised to discover that family vacations and traveling, especially going out of state were experiences mentioned most frequently. Disneyland and Disney World are the favorite vacation spots. Other important events included: flying; going to professional sport games; meeting somebody famous; winning awards; helping someone; seeing a baby born; being in love; and having sex. These favorite experiences often exemplified the comfort of family. The concept of being somewhere between a child and an adolescent and the feelings associated with this stage were demonstrated in these responses. But the overwhelming sentiment displayed was a desire to share more positive time with the family.

14. War is... Most responses were emotional with limited vocabulary such as: ugly; nonsense; unnecessary; killing; hell;

My favorite life experience is...

and *a tragedy.* Some thoughts were better articulated: *something very hurtful whose son might come home dead; people going out for us and dying for us; a fight that lasts a long time; when people from other countries battle against each other;* and *when people fight people.*

With the seventh and eighth graders more profound thoughts emerged: *a dispute in which only the strong survive; it's an excuse to kill people and mess up cities; adults who can't solve their problems peacefully; hateful; no winning; a lost cause; a power struggle; nothing to gain and everything to lose; a dummy game; a terrible misunderstanding between countries and people;* and *trying to overpower another country.* Both genders, various cultures, as well as different grade levels struggled with trying to define war.

15. My favorite book is... Some common books included: *Charlotte's Web, Where the Red Fern Grows, Misery, Superfudge, The Indian in the Cupboard, Sweet Valley Twin* series, Laura Ingalls Wilder book, *Hardy Boys* books, *Garfield,* sports biographies, and Stephen King novels. Again, there were no gender, cultural, or age boundaries in these statements. Eighth grade boys were as fond of *Secret Garden* and *Charlotte's Web* as girls were of *Indian in the Cupboard* and *Where the Red Fern Grows.* Comic books were still a favorite, especially with the boys. Girls did like the Babysitter Club books and romantic novels more than the boys did. Both genders enjoyed reading a variety of magazines, but the choices of magazines varied a great deal more for boys than girls. Some boys and girls mentioned they had no favorite books because they did not like to read.

16. My favorite movie is... *Home Alone One* and *Home Alone Two, Terminator* Movies, *Pretty Woman,* and *Don't Tell Mom the Babysitter's Dead* were most prominent. Favorite types of movies were slapstick, funny, horror, and romantic for the girls, and for the boys, silly, or action-packed thriller movies. Movies frequently cited were family focused and/or child centered. It

My favorite book is . . .

appeared that young adolescents enjoyed seeing kids their ages in situations unlikely to happen, but they would hope for responsibility, control, and power to resolve problems if the situations did happen to them. Girls cited romantic movies more than boys. While the boys did cite adventure movies more than girls, more boys mentioned romantic movies than girls did action packed movies.

17. My three favorite TV shows are... The responses overwhelmingly included: *Full House: Step by Step: Wonder Years; Blossom; Fresh Prince; Saved by the Bell; Simpsons; Family Matters; Baby Talk; Whose the Boss; Home Improvement;* and *Beverly Hills 90210.* Almost all TV shows were family based. (Young adolescents are like voyeurs who enjoy watching other families, comparing them and their problems and problem-solving techniques to their own families.) Seventh and eighth graders mentioned other shows like: *Rescue 911; FBI Most Wanted; Star Trek; Doogie Howser, M.D.; Alf; Coach; Murphy Brown; Quantum Leap; MacGyver;* and *Saturday Night Live.* Cartoons such as: *Ren and Stimpy; Garfield; Rug Rats; Doug; Bobby's World; Teenage Mutant Ninja Turtles; Tiny Tunes; Eek the Cat;* and *Beevis and Butthead* were popular with young adolescents.

18. My favorite color is... *Pink, black,* and *purple* seemed to be the favorites for fifth graders, upper grade girls liked *green* and *blue,* while the boys usually selected *black.* Neither boys nor girls had difficulty responding to this statement.

19. My favorite music is... Favorite music of middle school students included: *rap, rock, blues* and *alternative.* Although most love of music was for rock and rap, some students mention *Christian, classical, country,* and *jazz.* Boys did favor heavy metal and alternative music more than girls, and African Americans mentioned rap and jazz more frequently than others. The Beatles and Elvis were also highly recognized.

My favorite color is...

20.   My two favorite songs are... Girls had a greater variety of favorites that were more romantic and poetic than the music boys liked. The boys had a limited selection of favorites that were upbeat in rhythm and not as romantic as the slow dance kind. M.C. Hammer was popular at the time of this research, so *Pray, Two Legit to Quit* and *Can't Touch This* were popular for all populations.

21.   My favorite sport to play is... Almost all team sports such as basketball and volleyball were represented as well as individual sports like: *swimming, BMX bike riding, skiing, blading, gymnastics,* and *ice skating.* Team sports were mentioned by both genders although girls preferred more individual activities. Some boys indicated a preference for individual sports activities, but their common preferences were for team activities.

22.   The best thing about my age... Common responses by the fifth and sixth graders were: *get to do more; more freedom;* and *getting to participate in more activities.* Younger adolescents find more advantages about their age while older students in seventh and eighth grades felt more restrictions and more responsibilities while at the same time looking forward to the privileges of being older. Other responses included: *I get adult menus at restaurants; being tall enough to go on certain rides at parks; I'm becoming an adult; I am trusted more; next year I'll be in high school; two more years until I drive; oldest in school,* and *I am growing up but I am still a kid.* Responses of seventh and eighth graders don't applaud the new freedom expressed by the younger adolescents. They think their newly found freedom is lost to greater responsibilities. Most of the middle school students are positive and confident about their age relative to freedom and expectations. A large portion of the seventh and eighth graders look forward to getting their drivers' licenses.

23. The worst thing about my age is... Typical responses from fifth and sixth graders encompassed: *being caught between*

The best thing about my age is . . .

a grown-up and a kid; too young to go to some movies; can't ride certain rides; being the youngest in school; getting beat up; being younger than older brothers and sisters; getting made fun of; lack of respect; no one takes us seriously; getting ignored; going through puberty; six more years of school, and *more chores.* The seventh and eighth grade students responded: *too much homework; people don't take me seriously enough; I can't go on certain rides in parks; lack of trust; stress; too young; not liked by adults; too many limitations; not enough money; fights with siblings,* and *no one likes us.*

24.   Another age I would like to be is... The most common responses by all ages were: *16, so I can be old enough to drive.* A large proportion of the young adolescents wanted to be somewhere between 21-25 so they can be out of college; have a job; be able to vote; drink; and have a family. Several expressed an interest in being a certain age because of a cultural or religious celebration, while a large number also wanted to be younger so they can start life over and not make the same mistakes.

Some interesting gender variations were identified here. Girls wanted to be an age that focused on mature social behaviors like dating, driving, and hanging out with friends. However, boys, especially seventh and eighth graders, focused on careers, college, and other goals. Girls rarely stated such goals as frequently at any grade level. Other than religious and some culturally based celebrations and the dream of driving their own car, young adolescents really did not have many, if any, positive rites of passage to look forward to.

25.   What hasn't happened in your life you would like to happen... Most responses from both genders and all grades included: *meeting someone famous; going on a date; a first kiss; to travel* (especially abroad or out of state); *going to Disney World; getting rich; winning the lottery; getting a drivers license,* and *going to a World Series game.* Getting rich was important to all grades, although as girls became older, rather than getting rich

Another age I would like to be is . . .

themselves, they put greater reliance on marrying someone rich. Relationships with teachers, friends, and family were of greater importance to the girls than the boys. Sexual concerns were expressed by both genders in sixth, seventh, and eighth grades. However, boys thought of sex as "having it" and "doing it." While girls thought of having sex, they also thought of the potential outcomes of having a baby or getting a disease. Girls even as young as fifth grade frequently mentioned having a baby as being an experience that hasn't happened yet but they would like to have happen.

26. I would like to tell the President of the U.S... Boys and girls in fifth-eighth grades were concerned about the world they live in. These middle school students wanted to tell the President how to deal with a variety of problems including the environment, war, hopelessness, the economy, animal extinction, starvation in other countries, and educational funding. Responses from both genders, all ages, and regions were similar and usually fall under one of a variety of categories such as: *think more about all kinds of people; get out of office; reduce taxes; you did a good job; you did a poor job; do something about the environment; think about our country before other countries*, and *make the world a safer place.*

Culturally diverse populations and schools on the coasts gave more advice about poverty, ecology, and the need for the President to help our country before others.

27. The most important invention since I've been born is...

Such inventions mentioned since their birth consisted of: *Nintendo; Game Boys; VCRs; CDs; video games; computers; water parks; video cameras; hair spray;* and *microwaves.* Technological products were frequently mentioned by both genders. Boys focused more on video games and computers, while girls appreciated computers, telephones were mentioned more frequently. As the girls mature, hair spray and other grooming products were repeatedly specified. The young adolescents demonstrated they have no real time line of history to understand what precedes them. Other responses cited were inventions created long before their births.

The most important inventions ever... Responses consisted of: *electricity; indoor toilet; heating; ceiling fans; swimming pools; telephones; medicines; advances in medical science (penicillin); TVs; cars;* and *condoms.* An interesting range of thoughts, all of which presumably make life a little more comfortable.

28. I feel bad when... Young adolescents stated they usually felt bad when things weren't going well at school, at home, or with friends.

A preponderance of responses were: when I am *disliked; hated; yelled at; teased; made fun of; somebody is mean to me, picks on me or when I get poor grades on tests; I hurt my parents feelings; I get beat up; I hurt someone; I get bad grades; I am alone; I am rejected; mom and dad yell at me; teachers yell at me; my parents leave me alone; I have no money; I'm let down; a relative dies; I am not accepted for who I am; I let someone down; I am isolated;* and *I am misunderstood.*

Boys in fifth and sixth grades felt bad when they got in trouble, while the seventh and eighth grade boys felt bad when they did not do well in sports, or when their girl friends broke up with them. Boys also mentioned *hurting others, being hit,* or *hitting others* as making them feel bad.

Young adolescents on the coasts were more globally aware, and sensitive to contemporary issues than those students in the Midwest. There was little difference in these responses based on age, culture or gender. Concerns that make young adolescents feel bad involved: *seeing homeless people; that wars occur;* and *the uncertainty of the future of the world.*

29.   The last thing that made me feel bad was... *A relative dying; getting bad grades; getting into fights; being called a name; parents yelling; teachers yelling; not doing well on an athletic*

I feel bad when. . .

event; being mean to someone; having 2, 3, or 5 tests on a single day; and breaking up with a boy/girlfriend. Most responses were concerned with psychological events rather than physical ones, although physical problems were apparent when students mentioned getting hit or beaten, or being afraid of getting killed. Girls felt bad when egocentric things happen, like being yelled at, when their friendships are in jeopardy, and peer pressure.

30. I feel good when... They help people be nicer to each other; getting good grades; getting compliments; doing things with friends; sleeping; getting presents; test are canceled; parents do not yell; doing something good; brothers and sisters are not around; winning an event; doing something with the family; seeing others happy; listening to music; parents tell me they love me; not being called names; and I love; and I feel loved. Getting good grades and helping someone were equally important to all grade levels and both genders. Music became more and more important in helping the seventh and eighth grade students feel good. Sleep also played a role in helping young adolescents feel good, whether as a means of escape or to fulfill the needs of their growing bodies. Girls expressed a greater need for sleep at a younger age than the boys, possibly because of their earlier growth patterns. The events or possessions that make young adolescents in all populations feel good are very concrete.

The last time I felt good... Winning an award; getting good grades on a tests; being asked out; when a teacher did something nice; birthday parties; yesterday; going shopping; sleeping; and eating. Winning a sporting event or an award was important for both boys and girls. All populations indicated: enjoying recognition; getting compliments; being noticed by family, friends and teachers; going places; doing things with friends; and being with the family. Some young adolescents could not remember the last time they felt good.

31. To help myself feel better... Typical responses consisted of: run a mile; cry; talk to friends; play sports; scream;

I feel good when...

sleep; read; listen to music; walk around; eat; watch TV; play games; think; beat my pillow; play video games; nothing; write in my diary; play with pets; and *talk it out.* There was little difference in responses among the ages, but there were overt differences between genders. Girls, in some ways, were more solitary and conversational in making themselves feel better. Girls tended to talk about what was bothering them with a friend or parent, or they would read, talk on the phone, or cry. Boys, on the other hand, were more physical. They cited *participating in sports, hitting, playing Nintendo, hunting,* or *riding bikes.* Boys also mentioned *sleeping, eating,* and *watching TV* more than the girls to help them feel better. Boys didn't talk about their problems as much as girls. Some boys wanted to talk with their parents or friends but didn't or thought they couldn't. This lack of boys' ability to attempt to communicate is mentioned by both genders as one of the main characteristics that separates them.

It is apparent that most of the young adolescents have established a method to help themselves feel better, and most appear to be positive. Alcohol and drugs were not mentioned as behaviors used to help them feel better, but sex was.

32. If I could meet anyone living or dead, it would be _____ because... The most frequent response was *my grandfather,* followed by other relatives. Sports figures, especially Michael Jordan; singers; and actresses were also repeatedly mentioned. The President, Ross Perot, Franklin Delano Roosevelt, Albert Einstein, and God were frequently represented. Little difference was observed between genders and among grades except that girls more often mentioned wanting to meet males more than females. Boys also wanted to meet men more than women. A boy might mention meeting a female, if so, usually Christy Brinkley.

33. A friend is... Young adolescents of all ages thought that friends should be *trusting, loyal, honest, someone to hang out with,* and *caring.* Other responses included: *someone loyal to*

To help myself feel better...

you; trustworthy; nice; cares about you; friendly; honest; you tell secrets to; helps you; good listener; nice and funny; nice to you and doesn't fight; someone you can count on; caring, good values, understands you, and *listens to you.*

34. A best friend is... Young adolescents had a difficult time putting into words the difference between a friend and best friend. Frequently they said *like a friend but more.* Other responses were: *someone who helps you if you are hurt; a person you can trust and they trust you; you tell you deepest secrets to and share your feelings with; doesn't talk back; nicer than a friend; someone you can help during a tough time; someone you hang out with a lot; I can't explain; someone who comforts you; someone who understands you better than a friend* and *is always there,* and *always with you.*

35. The best thing about my gender is... These responses were at first most surprising, but after a while expected. Responses varied between ages and genders, but not ethnically. What fifth and sixth graders liked best about their genders were very concrete. For example, the girls at this age thought: *hair; makeup; being pretty; having long hair; going shopping; pretty things; being able to have babies;* and *looking sexy* were important. Boys at this age thought: *not being a girl; pro-sports; standing up to pee; not having to wear a dress; being stronger; able to do more things;* and *being bigger* were the best things. The seventh and eighth graders provided more abstract answers, although the boys still responded most frequently *not being a girl* and *being the best.* The boys did recognize that they: *have more opportunities; can do more things than girls; take things easier; that boys rule; our sports ability; no PMS; we are stronger;* and *we can't get pregnant.*

The seventh and eighth grade girls were not as confident or excited about their gender. They responded that the best things were: *looking pretty; the magic of having children; don't have to pay for dates; not having to do hard chores; we can wear every-*

A friend is . . .

thing; don't know, nothing; loving and caring; don't have to go to wars; going shopping, and *don't have to do hard things like boys.* The girls viewed the good things about their gender in terms of grooming and less physical work with such responses such as: *being pretty, hair* (the longer the hair the better), and *being restricted in that they do not have to do hard things.* The boys saw their gender as having greater advantages in a variety of opportunities, and did not focus on appearance as much as girls. These responses were apparent within all cultures. In brief, the best thing about being a boy is not being a girl and the best thing about being a girl is hair and being pretty. It was important that both genders viewed the value of their own gender as well as the value of the other gender.

36. The worst thing about my gender is... Whereas the boys had difficulty responding to this statement, the girls had no trouble responding to the worst about their gender. Girls responses included: *periods; PMS; wearing bras; boys say they can do everything better; people think I'm not as good as boys; lots of problems; can't be in sports; we don't have equal rights; puberty; messed up skin; sexism; having to have babies; getting pregnant,* and *all the dirty jokes about women.*

The boys rarely identified any negative aspects about their gender. But when strongly encouraged to respond they mentioned: *nothing; I don't know; we do all the work; it's awesome; different thoughts; nothing like being a boy; people blame us for all the stuff; having to buy condoms,* and *sometimes people don't think we are sensitive.*

Girls could clearly cite a large number of experiences they viewed as being negative based on gender. On the other hand boys were hard pressed to find negative things about being a boy. One thing that almost every class and every school had in common was that the word *gender* was known only by a few.

37. The biggest differences between the sexes is... The most common response was body parts. Concrete responses

The best thing about my gender is . . .

appeared in fifth and sixth grades and between genders. For example, the girls responded: *hair; having to lose last name when getting married; boys don't wear makeup; boys are more competitive; rights; boys are meaner; male ego; personalities* and *thought.* The fifth and sixth grade boys saw differences in: *height; no PMS; personalities; men are smarter; women wear makeup and men don't; hair; boys are better; sports; girls have babies; both think and act in different ways; a girl is gentle and a boy is not,* and *feelings.*

By seventh and eighth grade responses were more abstract in all populations. The boys responded: *girls have different feelings; the way we view things; attitudes; life; men are better than women; emotions; men are better; we act different; men are stronger and girls are pretty,* and *making love.* The girls' perceptions of the differences were not like the boys. Girls responded: *it's a man's world; how we grow up; what we do in our spare time; women's lib; boys don't express themselves as much as girls do; this is the world that gives males more opportunity; maturity level; guys get paid more; men don't have babies; the males think they are the head of everything;* and *girls are more sensitive.* Both genders recognized not only the biological differences between the genders but also opportunities, thoughts, and feeling.

38. In my free time I like to... *watch TV; read; play; go to the pool; go to the mall; ride bikes; what free time? draw; play with computer; play sports; listen to music;* and *play Nintendo or Game Boy.* Fifth and sixth grade students mentioned play more often than the older young adolescents. They saw play as something physical or recreational. By eighth grade play was barely mentioned by girls and when mentioned by boys it was usually to play a video game or to play a sport. The seventh and eighth graders sometimes said "Who has time to play?" Boys and girls were involved in many similar activities, although boys tended to do more physical things than girls. Culturally there were no real differences in what young adolescents choose to do.

39. My favorite joke is... Many of the jokes were just plain

In my free time I like to . . .

silly, and many were the same jokes told when I was a young adolescent. Knock, knock jokes were high on the list as were, variations of "Why did the chicken cross the road?" Boys, throughout the country, preferred dirty, bathroom, and blond jokes. However, boys in the Midwest seem to be more likely to tell racist and sexist jokes. In the coastal schools, some boys would apologize for telling racist jokes.

40. My favorite food is... Almost unanimously the favorite food of young adolescents was *pizza*. I asked them to be specific about what kind, but pizza was all I got. Other favorites included: *hamburgers, ice cream, macaroni and cheese*, and *chocolate chip cookie dough*. The seventh and eighth graders cited a greater variety and sophistication of foods, such as *crab with garlic butter, filet mignon*, and *Chinese, Italian*, and *Mexican*. Young adolescents of diverse cultures had a greater preference for food from their ethnic-based foods as well as foods of other cultures.

41. When I think of the future I... One response that always amazed me and was frequently cited was *flying cars*. Boys gave this response more often than girls. Other responses focused on: *having families; worry about ecology; afraid what the future will be like; I panic; think of world peace; think of wars; think of the world changing; technology; robots*, and *hope for more equal rights*. Gender perspectives were that boys thought about *college, war, family*, and *technology* and the girls saw the world in terms of *ecology, equity, family*, and *college*. For the most part feelings were divided in terms of fear based on ecology or hope based on family and technology. All populations demonstrated concern, worry, and stress about the future.

42. I worry about... Some interesting concerns were noted with little variation between genders, ages, and culture. The basic worries focused on: *family; the earth; politics; school;* and *friendships*. Frequently mentioned worries included: *making right*

When I think of the future I . . .

choices, pleasing others; growing up; getting bad grades; being poor; all the pressures; having a bad sickness; not having a boy/girlfriend; dying; earth not being here; pollution; crime; family; mother's job; war; my appearance; families; and divorce. Young adolescents worry a lot.

43. Language is... *a way to speak correctly; a class, speaking; words; foreign language;* and *communication.* I was disappointed that they viewed language so simplistically. They did not cite the retort "sticks and stones may break my bones but words will never hurt me." They know the power of language in this phrase through personal experience but they did not transfer it to a definition of language. In statement 28 being teased and called names were the most frequent contributions to making them feel bad, yet in this context young adolescents see language basically as a class.

44. A good teacher is... Young adolescents wrote: *A good teacher is one who makes the subject interesting; is nice; we have very few;* and *they care about their students.* Many middle school students thought a good teacher was someone: *who is not mean, who is caring; understanding; humorous; doesn't yell; doesn't have favorites; fair; makes learning fun; has a good sense of humor; you enjoy learning from,* and *doesn't give a lot homework.* The students articulated the need for teachers to be fair, honest, and nurturing to provide a positive learning environment. Homework for the sake of homework was acknowledged as different from homework with a purpose. Lecture and textbook type classes were not received positively from students. They were considered boring and ineffective. Advice given by middle school students: Nobody wants to walk into a room with a frowning teacher.

45. A good student is... Teachers have definitions of good students, but what qualities do young adolescents think a good student has? *Being attentive, good grades,* and *effort* were the

I worry about. . .

common responses. The fifth and sixth graders said: *someone who gets their homework done; behaves good in class; gets good grades,* and *does not give the teacher problems.* The seventh and eighth grade students supported many of the same qualities as their younger peers but also thought that good students were nice, friendly, caring, and care about the school. Girls viewed good students as being responsible, while boys generally saw a good student in terms of positive behavior, one who sits in his/her chair, and one who stays out of trouble.

46. A good principal is... *Someone who runs the school without problems; does discipline; someone who cares about staff, students, and teachers; knows the students; is seen around the school; someone who has fun but still gets the job done; gets involved with kids, caring, kind,* and *not a one-way thinker.* Hopefully these young adolescents' principals demonstrated such attributes. None of the students expressed knowledge of what principals do in terms of curriculum, instruction, or staff development. The young adolescents were generally naïve about what a principal does.

Young adolescents were only aware of possible leadership qualities in working with students and some working with teachers. Young adolescents thought that it is important for principals to check in on their teachers' classrooms and to hire good substitutes. Male and female principals were viewed differently. Women principals were thought to be sensitive and caring while male principals were thought to be less friendly, less flexible, and more strict.

47. My career goal is to... There was little difference in the responses between ages, gender, and culture, except that older males students were more specific. The responses from the girls included: *teacher; secretary; lawyer; judge; archeologist; work at NASA; pediatrician; cosmetologist; psychologist; journalist;* and *actress.* The most common response for girls was *being a veterinarian.* Boys' responses were more varied as indicated in these

A good student is...

replies: *Army, Air Force, Marine; astronaut; Supreme Court Justice; banker; political position; President; richest man in the world; architect; engineer; maker of video games; professional Nintendo player,* and *doctor.* The most frequent response for boys was *being a professional athlete.* Boys frequently mentioned dream jobs, while only a few girls mentioned being a model or actress. Boys thought in terms of the *Presidency, political offices,* and *engineers,* whereas girls did not. Boys' career goals were more lofty demonstrating greater self-confidence, whereas girls did not appear as confident in their goals and career selection.

48. My favorite subject is... Although almost all subjects were mentioned, the absolute most common responses by all grade levels and both genders were *math* and *science.* (Both math and science are concrete subjects; they deal with clear facts and concepts. Therefore their concepts may be more readily understood.) By eighth grade more interest in exploratories and electives were indicated.

49. My least favorite subject is... As in the previous statement all subjects were represented, this is no surprise: *language arts, social studies, English,* and *literature* are frequently cited as being the least liked. (Apparently young adolescents who are somewhere between the concrete and abstract cognitive levels of development find language arts, English, and social studies as less clearly defined and concrete.)

50. What I like best about school is... As expected middle school students liked school for social reasons. They liked: *seeing friends; lunch; recess; learning new things; nothing except friends; other kids; being around other people; going home; summer vacation; gives us something to do,* and *not having the same teacher every period.* Peer relationships and social interactions were easily observed as the value of school for young adolescents. Physical education, art, and music were also popular classes. Such classes require physical movement, which middle

My favorite subject is . . .

school educators know young adolescents need because of their growing bodies. Math class appeared frequently by all grades. Generally, fifth and sixth graders mentioned they like going to school to learn. Rarely did seventh and eighth graders say that learning was important to them. Both genders, and students from all geographical regions and cultures highly appreciate the social value of school.

51. What I like least about school is... Clearly, the two most common responses were *homework* and *it's boring*. Other thoughts were: *it's too long; going there; too much work; we don't have art or band; certain teachers; hours; some students who are bad; only one recess; sitting in a desk; we have so many classes; all the work; tests; reports; detentions; boring lectures; hard chairs; tension,* and *everything*. Specific classes and the expected work or tests of these classes were common responses. Seventh and eighth grade students mentioned boring classes frequently. All grade levels and boys in particular addressed school discipline procedures. Assertive discipline, demerits, or behavior modification were not favored by students.

52. My role model is... In addition to family members like *mothers, sisters, aunts, dads, uncles,* celebrities cited were *sports, movie, and/or TV stars. Michael Jordan* was the most frequent response. He crossed all age, gender, and culture boundaries. Boys identified celebrities more than girls. Elvis remained a hero to many. Relatives were most frequently mentioned by the girls.

53. Is there something I should have asked that I didn't? This question was asked because during the pilot study students would ask me why didn't I ask this or why didn't I ask that? Some of their questions became part of the statementaire, and this open question was added. It was important just to see what might be on their minds. Many of these responses were the issues young adolescents wanted to discuss, and other responses are less significant. Samples included: *Is there a heaven*

My role model is. . .

or hell? Do you guys take drugs? What's your favorite all-time toy? What's your favorite Nintendo game? Are you going to college? Who is your boy/girl friend? Where was I born? Do you know anyone with AIDS? You've asked just about everything. No, I really enjoyed taking this. Is school punishment accurate? Are you coming back? If you had one wish what would it be? Why am I here? You ask too much. I like having you here, are you coming back? If you could be in anyone else's' shoes, who would they be?

I am convinced by all the responses and from the questions raised in the open-ended last statement that young adolescents like inquiry. They like to question. They have profound thoughts and want to share their thoughts and develop new ones. Educators need to provide many opportunities for young adolescents to construct their thoughts, a forum for expressing them, and opportunities for them to explore and reflect on their thoughts. (Think how much we adults could learn.)

What we can learn is what we allow ourselves to learn from our young adolescents. It is important to believe that we can learn from them and that their thoughts are legitimate and need to be valued. Without an appreciation of young adolescents and their potential, it will be difficult to participate in a student-centered curriculum.

After reading these responses some readers might say, "interesting, but so what?" Such readers might close this book now and think they understand young adolescents better. But it is important that you delve into Chapters 3 and 4, discover the trends, and consider their curriculum implications. Then create a strategy for instituting a student inquiry curricula so you can learn the depth of young adolescent thought and have it reflected in your teaching. **v**

3.
Interpretations of Their Voices

The social realities of young adolescents that emerged from reading and reflecting on these responses led to insights that would be helpful in designing developmentally responsive educational programs. I established these categories to communicate the generalizations that grew out of their thoughts: *young adolescent development, young adolescents' perceptions of family,* and *young adolescents' perceptions of school.*

Young Adolescent Development

1) Care and caring are very important to young adolescents. Young adolescents wanted their parents, friends, and teachers to care about them and to demonstrate such caring. They frequently expressed wanting to help others to be more considerate and nicer to each other; wanting good teachers who care about their students; and believing that they care about their family and friends.

Being a caring teacher for these young adolescents involves being fair to all students, not showing favoritism, and maintaining control of the classroom. Students indicated that they get annoyed when teachers let some students get by with certain behaviors and not other students. Both male and female students addressed this concern.

2) Young adolescents have ambivalent feelings about the future. Two camps of thought on how young adolescents saw the future were observed – one of pessimists and one of optimists. This division was acknowledged through students' perception of technology. The pessimists worry about the future in terms of whether there will be one at all given nuclear power, toxic wastes, little recycling, and too much use of natural resources; the optimists thought in terms of technology and how it will enhance the future.

Pessimistic young adolescents who fear the future based their concern on the earth's population and the current inappropriate care it receives because of present technology. Young adolescents wanted to feel that they have some control over their futures, one based on the future of the earth.

A surprising response that appeared frequently in all grades and all schools from both genders was that when they think of the future they think of FLYING CARS.

3) Young adolescents believe the adult world does not like, appreciate, or understand them. Students mentioned that they thought grown-ups gave them little, if any, respect. They also revealed that some adults were afraid of them, particularly when they saw two or more kids walking down the street together. This saddens them. Young adolescents wish that grown-ups would try to understand them better and realize that things are different now.

4) Young adolescents realize the various ways their self-esteem is diminished. Some of the clearest trends identified in this project were that young adolescents are tired of: the adult world belittling their age group; teachers and parents yelling at them; friends making fun of them and other friends. They feel a need for developing inner peace. They recognized that conditions jeopardized how they feel about themselves and others. Young adolescents realized they are very much influenced by how others treat them. They know there are better ways of becoming productive individuals but feel they cannot control most of these factors.

5) Young adolescents feel good about themselves when someone says or does something nice for them and when they do nice things for others. When asked what makes them feel good, young adolescent responses were simple. They did not want to do big things or go to grand places, they simply wanted someone to say or do something nice to them or they wanted to do kind deeds for others. Certainly these are positive attributes for a group generally thought to be self-centered and egocentric.

6) Young adolescents are caught in an in-between time in their lives. They do not view themselves as children, but they are definitely not grown-ups or even late teenagers, and they know that. They are too big for rides in the kiddie park that they enjoyed last year. One day they go to a restaurant and get a kids' menu, the next day they get an adult menu. They get confused on this see-saw. They also think that this in-between status and the media coverage of their age group create an atmosphere that inclines toward disliking them. Because of this they do not believe they get the respect they deserve. The things that concern them are thought of as trivial by adults.

7) Young adolescents are fragile and their feelings are easily hurt. Young adolescent boys and girls expressed a need for their friends to stop teasing one another and hurting each other's feelings. They dislike the bad feelings that teasing creates and do not like being caught in the trap teasing establishes.

Students acknowledge that classmates contribute to much of the teasing they experience, but claimed that teachers are often guilty. Young adolescent voices often mention that teachers yell at them, make fun of them, and call them names. These behaviors hurt their feelings, make them mad, discourage them, and contribute to negative school experiences.

8) Fifth and sixth graders are more optimistic about being young adolescents than seventh and eighth graders. They liked the freedom associated with being in middle school. They think themselves to be more grown up, especially when they get their own lockers and participate in the "big people's" rides at water and amusement parks. As simplistic as these events appear to adults, they provide major messages and rites of passages to young adolescents growing up.

Even though seventh and eighth grade students liked the greater freedom, they feel they also have greater restrictions. They have more opportunities to do things, but are expected to behave in appropriate ways. They indicate they get mixed messages such as parents saying "It is okay to go on dates, but don't do anything." Young adolescents express an eagerness for even more freedom – when they go to high school and can start driving a car.

9) Young adolescents recognize they need space. Their bedrooms are very important places for them. They seek privacy and a chance to get away from all the confusion that society, schools, friends, and family deliver. In their bedrooms young adolescents can find some peace and just be themselves, at least for a little while. A seventh grade girl wrote, "Sometimes I need a little space to be my own person." For the many young adolescents without their own bedrooms, this becomes problematic, although the outdoors often includes a special spot.

Young adolescents need and should have opportunities to be alone, to think, to try to make sense of their social realities, family, school, and the world. A preschool child may hide in a corner or under a blanket, an adult might use the car as a place to unwind and think through a problem. Although young adolescents have the same needs, if not more so because of their developing lives, many have no space to call their own in which to collect their thoughts.

10) Young adolescents enjoy the process of constructing thoughts and knowledge. Young adolescents enjoy learning but wish that the process in school would be more exciting than what they currently experience. For the most part young adolescents found their educational experiences boring and lacking inspiration. However, when they had fair and caring teachers, an engaging curriculum, and some inspiration, students indicated they enjoyed school. Young adolescents liked for their teachers to challenge their thinking rather than just being asked to repeat information from textbooks and/or class lectures.

11) Young adolescents believe that they have a lot of pressure. They feel peer pressure, school pressure, home pressure, media pressure, and sports pressure. They feel they are expected to do good in everything and, as a result, become frustrated. Most young adolescents want good grades, to be on the honor roll, to play on certain teams, to look a certain way, to please their parents, and to fit in and conform. Many have high, unrealistic expectations of themselves and think they have to please everyone, everyone except one's own personal self. They become exhausted in these pursuits.

12) Differences in perceptions between cultures are less noticeable than those between the sexes. The most apparent cultural diversity pattern concerned students who lived on the coasts and attended more culturally diverse schools. These students were more closely connected to global concerns of poverty, ecology, hopelessness, and health issues than the young adolescents in the Midwest and those in less culturally diverse schools.

Hispanic and Latina girls seemed to be more sensitive and appreciative of the world around them than African American and white girls. Recent AAUW research (1992) shows that Hispanic girls have lower self-esteem than African Americans and white girls. *The Hostile Hallways* research (1993) states that more girls than boys in grades seven, eight, and nine first experience sexual harassment at school. African American (42%) and Hispanic (40%) girls first experience harassment prior to sixth grade compared to white girls at 31% (p. 22). Not only is it important to explore these two concepts in future research but to address these concerns daily in classrooms and hallways. Educators cannot turn their backs on incidents of verbal or physical harassment. This is particularly true for middle schools, as seventh grade is where the greatest amount of sexual harassment is experienced by both genders .

The gender perspective raised in this study is troubling. The attitude held by each gender clearly is different. Boys usually see the differences as related to physiology while girls relate the difference to a combination of sociological, psychological, physiological, and economic issues.

Fifth grade girls' responses indicate they view their gender in physical appearance and biological processes. As girls mature their thinking becomes more abstract regarding gender issues. They are beginning to realize they are treated differently; perceived differently; experience different expectations; have different responsibilities in life with fewer options and limited economic opportunities, as well as having greater restrictions.

Fifth grade boys, like the girls, view their gender in concrete terms like physical pain (getting kicked or picked on), having greater strength, or what they wear. As the boys entered the formal level of cognitive development they see their gender as being more intelligent, having more opportunities, having more fun, and having a more demanding workload.

The 13 and 14 year-old girls expressed gender difference in such terms as: *it's a man's world; guys tend to take advantage of us; PMS; boys have greater opportunities and seem to get ev-*

erything. Pubescent boys view gender difference in terms of physical sexuality: *girls have breasts; boys don't have a period; and girls have to worry about getting pregnant.* Boys frequently used derogatory terms describing girls' body parts.

Girls were concerned with biological activities ranging from: *having periods; getting their periods at school; PMS; worrying about having babies; the pain of childbirth;* to *having the pride that they can have babies.* Girls expressed the notion that they have a lot of things to worry about while trying to learn social studies, language arts, and other academic pursuits.

It appeared to both the boys and girls concluding their first decade of life and starting their second decade that there is no significant advantage to being a girl. This identified trend supports what other studies have already established about being a boy or a girl (AAUW, 1992, 1993, 1995; Gilligan et al., 1989; Gilligan & Mickel-Brown 1993; Riley et al. 1993; Sadker & Sadker, 1982, 1993).

In this research study both the boys and girls thought that boys can do more, are viewed differently, have different expectations, have different restrictions, and have greater opportunities. The boys thought of themselves as having a great deal to enjoy by being a boy. They found few problems with being one and viewed the biggest difference as biological, with different restrictions and expectations.

The girls, on the other hand, were hard pressed to find good things to say about being a girl, but readily identified a variety of negative things about being one. Although the girls were aware of the different biological expectations and responsibilities between genders they saw the biggest difference to be in opportunities. The average middle school girl thought that boys can do more now, will be able to do more as they grow up, have fewer restrictions, have higher status career expectations, and will probably get paid more.

With both middle school boys and girls the perception is that being a girl is not nearly as special as being a boy. When the boys gave such a response during the dialogue sessions other boys would laugh, and some of the teachers also laughed. Girls did not appreciate the display of humor and were visibly offended by the laughter and what was said. There were a couple occasions in which girls said "I know what boys will say. They think the best thing about being a boy is not being a girl."

13) Girls think survival techniques are important to know; boys regard knowledge and how to do things as important to know. What girls found important to know included survival skills: friend selection, the need to say no, safe sex, and staying out of alleys. The boys valued: having skills; knowing how to do things; having and accomplishing goals; and reading and math.

14) What young adolescents do in their free time varies considerably. Free time is important for young adolescents because it is during this time they get to do things they like to do. It is expected that young adolescents would participate in various activities from reading, sports, to watching TV – all of which they do. However, two common responses provided were play and sleep, two important elements in the life of a young adolescent.

15) Sleep is important for young adolescents. Frequently young adolescents addressed a need for sleep. They sleep to help themselves feel better; they sleep in their free time; and they sleep because their bodies need it. Young adolescents recognize that sleep is important for their growth and development.

16) The concept and practice of "play" is eliminated as fifth graders and sixth graders mature into seventh and eighth graders.
More fifth graders responded to play than other grades. But by the time young adolescents reach sixth or seventh grade, they have greater time restrictions and play takes a back seat. If an eighth grader mentioned play it was usually a boy and connected to a specific kind of play such as "play Nintendo," "play basketball", or "play music." Giving up play time was a rite of passage, noticed by some but not recognized by others.

17) Fifth grade girls are more active physically than older middle school girls. They tend to favor participation in various sports to a greater degree than the sixth, seventh, and eighth graders. The older girls seem to prefer music, reading, or shopping, again possibly because they are in the middle of the growth spurt and may feel less coordinated and have a greater need to develop social relationships. The eighth grade girls mentioned the mall and shopping as important parts of their lifestyle.

18) Boys have a variety of celebrated role models while girls note very few celebrated women as role models. Julia Roberts was frequently cited. Both boys and girls identified Michael Jordan as their model. Girls generally chose mothers, aunts, sisters, and friends to be their role models. Boys almost exclusively chose sports figures as their role models. Sometimes boys would chose a rock and roll star or Einstein as someone to emulate.

Career goals responses also reflect different visions between genders. A large percentage of boys look forward to glamour jobs, such as professional sports without a reality check on the possibility of having the talent or luck to achieve such status. A few girls, usually fifth and sixth graders, think of becoming models or actresses, but for the most part girls saw themselves as mothers, teachers, veterinarians, physicians, and attorneys.

19) When wanting to meet someone, most young adolescents select a relative, often a grandparent who had died. This is part of the family connection that young adolescents appear to value. Often their interests were based on a desire to meet that relative because they had been told that they reminded others of that person. Young adolescents are curious about their connections to the past and to their families. It was encouraging to note how much young adolescents value their families, even more highly than celebrities.

20) Hair is important to young adolescents. Girls value hair and think it is one of the best things about a girl. Generally, the longer the hair, the better. Hair is a means for young adolescents to conform or not conform, of being creative, or following image makers, or taking a stand. For young adolescents, hair, its length, and style is a gauge of appearance, image, and status.

21) Girls write longer responses and in greater detail than boys. Girls had more in-depth responses. Boys' responses were limited to a few words, were concise, and to the point. Similar behaviors were experienced in my conversations with the students. Girls did not speak as loudly or as assertively as the boys, nor as frequently.

22) Trust is important to young adolescents. Middle school students want to be able to trust teachers, friends, and parents. And they want teachers, friends, and parents to trust them. They indicated an interest in learning skills useful in developing trust in their own behaviors and towards others. It hurt them that adults assume young adolescents will act in irresponsible and distrusting ways.

23) Young adolescents want to communicate with adults. Young adolescents want open communication with their teachers and want to engage in real dialogue about their learning and life in general. They express a desire to have some influence over what they are to learn and how they might learn it. Young adolescents do not see school as belonging to them and want to contribute and connect with their learning environment.

Young adolescents also want to communicate openly and honestly with their parents and want to express themselves and talk about what they do, how they do, about their friends, or lack of friendships. They want to talk about what hurts them and why it hurts and to share what makes them feel good and why, to tell parents how they do in school. They want to talk about what is going on in the world and what it means to them now and in the future. They want to talk about the future, their concerns about it and whether there will be one, and how they can influence their individual futures as well as the future of the world.

Young adolescents also want more open and honest relationships with their friends so they can tell them to stop being mean to them and to others, to stop calling people names, to stop calling on the phone, and to give them space. These students also want their friends to know how important they are to them.

24) Young adolescents do not connect the concept of language to how words impact people. I thought that young adolescents would pick up on the power of language and how it is used, but I was disappointed. Since they had often expressed concern over the amount of name-calling and yelling in their lives and because their age group gets hurt and picked on by others through words, I expected the power of language to be a concept they possessed. Although they are very connected to the pain that words can bring, when asked about language they saw it as a class, a foreign language, or a form of communication.

25) Young adolescents have not developed an adult concept of time. When identifying their favorite inventions the students thought that many known innovations had been invented during their lifetime. They were confused about when something had been invented in relation to their lives. It was as though modern progress had only occurred since they had been born.

26) Young adolescents value their pets. Pets were mentioned more in terms of friendships than as responsibilities. Pets play a central role in the lives of young adolescents, serving as non-judgmental listeners. When young adolescents feel a need to hug someone or need someone to talk to, their pets provide them comfort. It is a tragic time in a young adolescent's life when a beloved pet dies.

27) Young adolescents focus on God and Jesus in a variety of responses. In addition to the family connection a religious and spiritual connection was also represented. God and Jesus were equally represented throughout the country, across grades, culture, and gender. Some young adolescents recognize their spiritual side and feel comfortable with it.

28) Young adolescents are media consumers. They enjoy TV, music, movies, videos, MTV, and magazines. They believe they learn about themselves and how to become what they are through media. They expressed the belief that the media provided information about issues they couldn't get elsewhere. *YM* and *Seventeen* magazines are particular favorites.

29) Young adolescents strongly favor family situation comedies when viewing TV. They love family shows. Some students mentioned talk shows, and a few students mentioned that they enjoy watching MTV, but these were not as high a priority as were situation comedies. Many students may not have had access to MTV, and that is partly why it wasn't as high a viewing preference.

Young Adolescents' Perception of Family

1) Young adolescents worry about family members, death, divorce, violence, and the condition of the earth. They are highly concerned about whether there will be a world in that future, and if so what kind of world will it be. They face worries daily that, for the most part, were nonexistent during previous generations when their parents and teachers were growing-up.

Young adolescents worry about their parents' health, jobs, divorce, and possible deaths. There appears to be an underlying feeling of uncertainty about a secure family unit. Young adolescents also fear some form of violence happening to them, their friends, and/or family. Since violent acts are often random, these children fear and feel that something can happen to them or someone they love at anytime, anywhere.

2) Young adolescents enjoy being with their families and would like more family time. The favorite life experiences expressed by the young adolescents were family vacations or other adventures with the family. It is encouraging for families to know that young adolescents enjoy spending time in family activities and express a desire to spend time with parents.

3) Mothers are more influential in the lives of young adolescents than fathers. Young adolescents express more concern about mom and compliment her and acknowledge more affection toward her than toward dad. They demonstrated a great pride when mom acquired a new job. Mothers appeared as strong role models for both sons and daughters who spoke proudly of their mothers. It is desirable that young adolescents respect and feel good about their mothers, but it is a concern of parents, educators, and citizens alike that fathers seem to have lost a position of prominence in the lives of young adolescents.

4) Young adolescents want to tell their families that they love them, but... They want to affectionately communicate with their parents even though perceived barriers seem to preclude it. They recognize the support and love that parents have provided and wish that they could tell their parents how they feel but were not comfortable approaching their parents with this affection.

5) Young adolescents sincerely dislike their siblings. Whether the siblings were younger or older, and whether this is a passing phase or not, young adolescents readily demonstrated a strong dislike for their brothers and sisters. If the siblings were younger, the older siblings felt they have these tagalongs and that their brothers/sisters get in the way. If the young adolescents were the younger siblings, they appeared to get beat up physically and/or emotionally by their older siblings on a regular basis. If they were the middle children they experienced these problems from both sides. As one middle level student wrote "My little brother's bugging me, and then I get mad and hit him. Then I get blamed for it. Or when my older brother's acting all macho and trying to pick on me. I wish my brothers would disappear." He was not alone in this line of thinking.

Young Adolescents' Perceptions of School

1) Grades are a major concern for young adolescents. Grades appear to influence the self-esteem of young adolescents and create pressures for them. They feel good about themselves when they get good grades; they feel bad about themselves when they get poor grades. They worry about the implications that their grades have for college and careers. Grades and homework create a great deal of stress for a majority of students and appear to be a constant thorn in their sides.

2) Young adolescents do not like homework, especially if it is not relevant. They consider homework to be busywork. For many students homework was a major stressor. Such students may have special needs, family responsibilities, an excess amount of homework, a busy schedule, or a combination of factors that affect their completing homework.

Students could not understand why they often have several tests and/or projects due the same day or the same week. They didn't understand why teachers couldn't work things out so that assignments would not be due simultaneously. Middle school students were quick to suggest that teachers should confer with each other to know what other teachers are doing, and coordinate dates for major assignments or tests. This is one thing teaming should correct, and young adolescents themselves saw the need for this aspect of teaming.

3) Middle school students want to share school issues, grades, and other school concerns with parents. I was surprised how often students wanted to tell their parents the grades they got on tests, but didn't. They also indicated they want to share personal things that happen to them at school and concerns they have about other family members.

4) Young adolescents have a strong sense of fairness. Students often mentioned that some teachers show favoritism to particular students. In some schools one gender thought that the other gender got preferential treatment. Young adolescents view favoritism as providing opportunities and experience for some students while ignoring others. They identified such poor practices as calling on some students but not others, ignoring the behavior of some while paying too much attention to others, yelling at some kids but not at others. Students want an orderly, organized, fair classroom; and they know when such a classroom isn't in place.

5) Young adolescents do not understand what principals really do. Students knew who their principals were, but not exactly what they did. Students felt the difference in a school that had a nurturing leader as compared to one that had an authoritarian leader. Principals that were visible, caring, and gave hugs, had a positive effect on the school as well as on the individual students. A comfort level was identified by the respondents. However, where the principal was more of an authoritarian, students did not feel as comfortable. They thought such principals were mean, not caring. Students cited a fear of going to school where they felt uncomfortable.

Middle school students also thought that it was important for principals to check in on teachers more often to see what was going on in the classroom. They perceived that some teachers frequently practiced certain negative behaviors, ones students deemed as inappropriate.

Young adolescents suggested that teachers and principals need to choose substitute teachers more carefully. They want good "subs" who will not let them get by with stuff.

6) Fifth through eighth graders perceive differences in the qualities of a good student. Fifth graders thought a good student was one who just gets good grades and behaves in class. Older middle school students thought of a good student in more complex terms such as one who displays good behaviors, is nice, does homework, listens, pays attention, and does not give teachers grief. Some mentioned that good students are simply those who sit in their chairs.

7) Middle grades kids listen to inner voices. Young adolescents put on internal tapes in their minds and play them over and over: "Why are you so clumsy? Can't you do anything right? Can't you get organized? How many times do I have to tell you? Why can't you remember to bring your books? How can you be so stupid?" They hear these phrases time after time from parents, teachers, and even peers and then unfortunately buy into them and believe they are true. Young adolescents' beliefs in the possible validity of these statements and hearing them said repeatedly affect their self-esteem.

Summary

These generalizations about young adolescents quickly emerged from the vast number of responses gathered in this study. Collectively they paint a self-portrait of young adolescent culture. We see their views of self, their friends, their school environment, their families, and the adults in their lives. These revealing thoughts can and should enhance adult perceptions of young adolescents and influence how we teach and parent them.

Educators can support the maturation of young adolescents by designing developmentally appropriate curricula, advisory, enrichment, and exploratory activities. We do not have to create new programs. All we need to do is provide students opportunities to think and develop confidence in their thoughts; time, places, and methods to assist them in articulating their thoughts; and chances to connect their ideas and interests to the schooling experience. **V**

4.
Curriculum Implications of Young Adolescent Voices

I once read about a teacher who came to class with a large jar full of marbles. The teacher challenged the class to guess how many marbles were in the jar. The students could only look at the jar as the teacher held it. They couldn't get close to it, hold it, or even touch it. A teacher down the hall entered a classroom with a similar size jar filled with the same kind of marbles and asked the students how many marbles they thought were in the jar. These students were then allowed to touch the jar, move the jar around, measure the jar, hold the jar, and weigh the jar. They could ask questions and bring in other marbles and jars to compare. The students could try a variety of ways to concoct an answer. The teacher wasn't concerned merely with getting the right answer; she was more interested in having her students explore, construct, connect, and discover. She encouraged her students to bring their thoughts and experiences into the classroom.

The students in the first class were denied such learning avenues. The only person in that classroom who had the correct response was the teacher, and the only way the students could learn how many marbles were in the jar, other than a wild guess, was for the teacher to tell them. Which class made the best estimates? Which class had more learning occurring? Which class would you want to attend?

Some teachers, figuratively speaking, know how many marbles are in the jar and will only allow students to find out by telling them. They teach as though only they hold the key to knowledge and what they want students to learn are the only important things to know. Other teachers share their knowledge and experiences and let the students share their knowledge and experiences as well. They build learning onto what is important and familiar to the students. Together the students and teachers discover the "number of marbles in the jar."

The discovery process involves the teacher as a learner in the process. They and/or their students present a problem, a concern, an issue to be investigated, and they seek to solve the problem together. All involved in the process learn and value each other's thoughts and learning processes. What is learned is that there are many ways to solve a problem. The students learn that knowledge is connected to them in some personal way. It then becomes relative and active, related to what is going on in their lives. Because the learning process is both an active and authentic one, what is learned is not merely stored for use later in life or for a test, but is to be used as young adolescents become distinctive young adults.

This style of learning is not new, it is what John Dewey advocated at the beginning of the 20th century. He recognized the need for school curricula to have a symbiotic relationship between the experiences and knowledge of children and the experiences of society as organized into school content. Since society today is more diverse and complicated than the one familiar to Dewey, the need is now even greater for connecting students' experiences and knowledge to the school curricula.

Educators can no longer expect that the comfort and boundaries of textbook and pre-planned courses of study sufficiently encompass what it takes to educate students. Such approaches to curricula deny teachers their individual intellectual, creative, and professionally honed abilities – a great loss for the sake of convenience. Educators need to capture and maintain their individual pedagogical perspectives, personally explore the culture of the young adolescents they teach, and then let the results of their exploration become apparent in their class content and methodology.

Paulo Freire (1982) likened education to a banking system. Teachers deposit information in the minds of students as they would money into a bank, and then at various points teachers withdraw some of this knowledge by giving tests, like going to a bank and withdrawing money. This is not the kind of education that Dewey and others in the progressive education movement advocated for an effective student-centered curricula during the first quarter of the 20th century. They championed such concepts as:

- Start where the learners are, then build on their strengths.

- School experiences should be relevant to the learner and his/her felt needs.
- Children learn by doing and need to be active in the learning process.
- School is not a preparation for life; it is life, so school experiences should be functional and useful for children while they are engaged in the learning process.
- Educational activities should be integrated around problem solving and inquiry.
- Classrooms should be democratic so that children learn how to participate in democracy and in social groupings.
- School curriculum should satisfy the personal needs of all learners while it serves the needs of society. It should be diverse yet provide a common, unifying experiences.

(Goodman, Bird, & Goodman, 1991)

These concepts are essential to a student-centered inquiry-based curriculum. Interestingly, such educational ideals are highly visible and relatively traditional in a good preschool or kindergarten class. Observe a dynamic preschool program and you will see theme teaching, learning stations, rest time, snack time, recess, hands-on learning, cooperative learning, multi-age groupings, advisory activities, parent involvement, music, humor, and evaluations – but no grades! Students learn at their own rates and are not academically compared to other students in the class but experience a curriculum based on knowledge of students' prior experiences and their interests, conditions that lead to success. Preschoolers are encouraged to learn through a "marble-jar" approach, learning in a truly student-centered and inquiry-based environment. Why does schooling take such a dramatic shift once formal schooling has begun?

When students are learning in marble jar style they are bringing the knowledge, questions, and concerns that James Beane addresses in *A Middle School Curriculum: From Rhetoric to Reality* (1993). Beane strongly advocates using an intersection of personal concerns and social issues to determine curriculum themes. He writes:

> In the intersections between these two categories {personal concerns and social issues}, then, we may discover a promising way of conceptualizing a general education that serves the dual purpose of addressing the personal

issues, needs, and problems of early adolescents and the concerns of the larger world, including the particular society in which they live. It is here that we may find the themes that ought to drive the curriculum of the middle school as a general education program. And it is here that we may finally find a way of positioning subject matter so that it presents a justifiable and compelling source of study for early adolescents and the adults who work with them. (p.60)

It is my belief that these themes need to be based on the voices and thoughts of young adolescents acquired through inquiry. As themes for class study are created in your class they must be done with full student participation. (I use the term trends rather than themes, fearful that themes may become too simplistic or not reflect conditions that make each school population unique.)

The student voices heard in this project formed various generalizations that were presented in Chapter 3. The same categories of the generalizations provide the framework for discussing the curriculum implications of the findings.

Curriculum Implications in the Area of Young Adolescent Development

1) Care and caring are very important to young adolescents. As young adolescents seek to make sense of the world around them, it is important that they have a positive, caring, and confident foundation on which to build their world view and self-understanding. They may be encouraged to behave in cooperative caring ways, but are expected to live in the competitive world of grades, sports, and social relationships. While forming their attitudes, morals, and values, they are constantly exposed to conflicting values and standards in school and in life. Yet the personal decisions they make may become lifelong values. Middle school students need guidance,unbiased knowledge, and opportunities to reflect in order to complete this critical developmental task confidently and satisfactorily.

Educators and parents should be positive role models of caring behaviors. If young adolescents are exposed to a humanitarian environment then they will emulate such practices themselves. Adults frequently complain that children lack social consciousness and treat others with disregard. Adults can help counter this behavior by creating and practicing in a caring environment.

Every day in some way practice caring behaviors. Young adolescents are surrounded daily by a flood of violent and antagonistic messages. Peers, teachers, and even family members may pick on them; the media are filled with images of brutality, while our students are longing for a kind word from someone.

I was surprised by the large number of respondents who said their teachers would frequently yell at students and tell their classes to shut-up and sit down. It is important for teachers to put themselves in the shoes of students and imagine how they would feel if they were treated as some students are treated in schools every day.

Teachers and parents need to break the petty harassment cycle and stop buying into the theory "kids will be kids" and "that's part of this age," or "boys will be boys." As long as adults support these beliefs, young adolescents will view the resulting behaviors as approved.

Even if it is no more than a smile or a kind comment, young adolescents need evidences to indicate they are cared for. According to the student responses in this project, a good teacher could be defined primarily as a caring and understanding person. *So relax, step back from the stress and hurried schedule you have as a teacher and demonstrate that you care about your students and that you enjoy just being with them.* All the subject matter you try to impart will not replace the importance of your caring about your kids.

2) Young adolescents have ambivalent feelings about the future. They believe that they will live in the future, yet they fear it, because they see a violent society rapidly changing through technology and environmental issues. This uncertainty confuses them. Schools need to provide young adolescents opportunities to address their uncertainties. Students should be helped to develop goals, set sights, and plan for the future.

Prepare students for the future by having them become: 1) globally aware, 2) technologically literate, 3) involved in opportunities for proactive community service focusing on ecology with direct action improving their community, and 4) masters of the skills needed to achieve their goals. Such skills and behaviors can be addressed in the curriculum through having technology, environmental concerns, and community service activities infused throughout the curriculum. Students will then see their school-work as relevant and related to the community.

3) Young adolescents believe that the adult world does not like, appreciate, or understand them. Thy perceive that adults assign them little status. This may then contribute to the low self-esteem that burdens many middle school students. Young adolescents have a strong perception that adults do not take them seriously.

They dislike the stereotypical expressions about their age, such as "out of control," "difficult time," and "walking hormones." They find such expressions offensive. It is important that educators not denigrate this age, however innocently, by describing it with generalizations that are negative. This is a serious concern for them, therefore it should be for us as well. *Value students and demonstrate your respect for them.* Learn about their growth and development, avoid making fun of them, don't use sarcasm, but in all ways demonstrate that you value their thoughts and understand their concerns.

4) Young adolescents realize the various ways their self-esteem is diminished. How one feels about him/herself greatly influences learning. A survey of literature estimated that over 10,000 scientific studies have been conducted on self-esteem and that there are over 200 different tests used to measure self-esteem (Adler, 1992). The report *How Schools Shortchange Girls* (AAUW, 1992), demonstrates the loss of self-esteem that both middle school boys and girls experience. The loss levels off for boys but continues throughout high school for girls. According to the report, this loss of self-esteem influences the courses selected in high school, which in turn influences college and related lifelong decisions. (Many teachers have poor self-esteem and need to work on improving it. As teachers involve students in a variety of self-esteem activities, they should be encouraged to participate themselves.)

Students are aware of times they lose self-esteem and times when it is enhanced. *Avoid activities that pit students against one another, avoid negative or sarcastic comments, and provide opportunities in which students can help one another.*

5) Young adolescents feel good about themselves when they do nice things for other people. Students like to help and be nice to others and vice-versa. Teachers can assist students in feeling good and being happy simply by making positive comments when warranted, doing little things for them, and creating opportunities for them to do something nice for others. Imagine how much educators could change the school environment simply by practicing kindness and niceness!

Establish effective short term and long lasting community service projects, and practice everyday acts of kindness. Behaving generously toward others helps us feel good about ourselves. Competition undermines caring and kindness and teaches us to look out for number one rather than others. In competition some individuals develop a fear of losing position or status. The more competitive individuals become the less likely they are to be generous. *Balance opportunities for kindness and generosity with competitive activities.*

A current movement popularized by Ann Herbert (1993) is the practice of Random Acts of Kindness, which involves individuals spontaneously doing something kind for someone else such as putting money in an expired meter of another's car, paying the toll charge of the car behind you, taking cookies to a hospital or nursing home staff. *Kids' Random Acts of Kindness* (1995) is a resource to help generate activities for students. Family random acts of kindness also should be encouraged in order to become part of a child's lifestyle.

Community service projects can be implemented in any class and/or as part of advisory. Activities may include planting a flower garden on school grounds with each class being responsible for a section. Occasionally the flowers can be picked and given to senior citizens, school staff, or parents. Students can maintain a school vegetable garden, which also yields many benefits and lessons.

With simple positive teacher behaviors and a curriculum infused with community service activities it is easy to help young adolescents be positive and optimistic. And when students have a good attitude, they will learn more and enjoy learning. Although some teachers may not think it is their job to make students happy, it is their job to help students succeed, and the two are closely interrelated.

Even though students have historically always been educated in a competitive format, that doesn't mean competition is a good way for all students to learn. *Avoid highly competitive classroom activities. Competitive programs do not encourage kindness.* Competition separates students into those who like to compete and those who do not like to compete. When these non-competitive students are placed in a curriculum activity that promotes competition, they are placed in a compromising and uncomfortable situation.

6) Young adolescents are caught in an in-between time in their lives. Some of the reasons students liked being young adolescents were also thought of as drawbacks as they grew older. For both the best and worst things about their ages young adolescents had no difficulty responding. They saw themselves on a see-saw in life trying to balance the need to be alone and needing and wanting to be with their families. They like their friends one minute, and the next minute find themselves making fun of them, then feeling guilty about their behavior. They like the freedom of being older but find it difficult to accept the greater responsibilities. They appreciate having higher expectations but resist the different kinds of restrictions placed on them. *Understand this see-saw nature of early adolescents, respect it, and try to help balance it.* It is important for adults who recognize these dual needs of young adolescents to try and make them feel good about themselves as they seek to establish balance. Help ease the pain and frustrations of young adolescents by not referring to them as "hormones with feet" or "the range of the strange."

Young adolescents are trying to become more independent yet still need the comfort and security provided by parents and other significant adults. The independence that young adolescents seek sometimes presents them with difficult decisions they may not be equipped to handle. *Provide opportunities for real dialogue and allow students to be open and comfortable with you.* Frequently young adolescents recognize their inability to make some decisions but are afraid to seek advice from adults for fear of being viewed as a child. Recognize that young adolescents still need some of the comforts and warmth that childhood provides. *Have special areas with stuffed animals where young adolescents can go to feel like it's okay to be a kid.*

7) Young adolescents are fragile and their feelings are easily hurt. They feel a lot of pain, pain created by what parents, siblings, friends, and teachers say, do, or imply. Educators cannot turn their backs on incidents of verbal or physical harassment. If we expect young adolescents to act in a civil manner, so must we. Students mimic behaviors of their teachers, so avoid yelling, teasing, or using sarcasm. Some adults may think students like sarcastic put-downs, but they don't.

Getting "picked on" is equally disturbing to both boys and girls in all cultures and grade levels. How can we expect young adolescents to commit themselves to learning in school when they have so much discomfort? AAUW's *Hostile Hallways* (1993), studied the frequency and types of harassment experienced by school age children. According to the study the two most frequent places young people are harassed are in the school hallways and the classrooms. Young adolescents should feel safe in the school they are required to attend. This AAUW research also states that the highest amount of sexual harassment experienced throughout the K-12 schooling process in in the seventh grade. We cannot ignore or pretend we do not see harassing behaviors. Give young adolescents confidence by making it clear that harassing behaviors are not to be tolerated and that it is not permissible to act in crude or inappropriate ways. *Establish a district harassment policy, have it sent to families, discuss it in class at the beginning of the school year, revisit it upon occasion, post it in your classroom, and act when you see any form of harassing behavior.* Don't fail to help a student being harassed emotionally or physically.

Middle school students are at the turning point of their lives, so it is important that they have ample opportunities to develop fully as individuals without being trapped by preconceived notions or old attitudes. Educators are responsible for helping both boys and girls succeed in a non-sexist classroom and curriculum and by providing a safe haven from any form of harassment or bias.

8) Fifth and sixth graders are more optimistic about being young adolescents than seventh and eighth graders. Fifth and sixth graders like their new freedom with few new responsibilities. Seventh and eighth graders have already outgrown their fifth and sixth grade freedom and want more but face new restrictions. They want to drive and date and hang out. It is also important to understand that young adolescents don't fully understand these feelings and therefore often cannot articulate how or what they feel. They are still children becoming young adults. Schools are often guilty of providing activities that encourage young adolescents to grow up too fast. *Eliminate or limit the number of "adult like" activities your school sponsors such as: formal graduation exercises, dances, and superlatives.*

9) Young adolescents recognize they need privacy and space. Kids often say "I need space." They feel a need for both physical and psychological space. They view space as a need, not just something they want. Middle schoolers seek time away from others to reflect and try to make sense out of their own lives. *Provide "cubbies" in your classroom or school where young adolescents can escape for a few minutes.* In those spaces young adolescents can connect their childhood with their adolescence. Just as toddlers need a time-out, so do young adolescents. They do not always consciously recognize this need and may act out in an inappropriate fashion when that need can't be met.

10) Young adolescents enjoy the process of constructing thoughts and knowledge. When students bring their experiences to the classroom and teachers help them connect these experiences to the material being studied, students are then "constructing knowledge." Not only do they learn to construct knowledge but they also to learn to think. These abilities contribute to the development of self-confidence that leads to positive self-esteem and a love of learning. *Challenge students' thinking and allow them to construct their own thoughts rather than having them just repeat information.*

Recall the delight of children when playing with building blocks. They create and use their imaginations to construct bridges and buildings. The same individuals who once constructed bridges can now construct knowledge when provided the opportunity.

11) Young adolescents believe that they have a lot of pressure on them. They feel pressure from parents, siblings, friends, classmates, and teachers. They put pressures on themselves by wanting to please others, participating possibly in too many activities so they can fit in or excel. They are pressured by media images of perfection that cannot be achieved. Grades and honor rolls provide added pressures because some young adolescents feel a need to prepare for the "best" college or the "right" career. *Monitor the number of school activities students are al-*

lowed to join and the types of assignments and projects assigned. Avoid placing so much emphasis on "when you get older you will need to" or "wait until next year..." It is important we allow young adolescents to be who they are now in order for them to be their best selves in the future. We do not need to rush them through their childhoods. Young adolescents shouldn't have to take on the world and the future now.

12) Differences in perceptions between cultures are less noticeable than gender perceptions. What was an interesting but not an unexpected discovery in this research was how the perceptions of life and learning are defined by gender more than culture.

Some geographic differences were reflected in dissimilar perceptions on socioeconomic and ecological issues. Educators cannot be expected to understand all the variations of viewpoints, but it is important and necessary to explore them to see how such deviations effect world peace, ecology, economics, opportunities, housing, careers, and other components of life. *Connect what is presented in textbooks and media to what happens daily in the lives of students; explore, invite, read between the lines, critique all forms of media, and try to identify and eliminate possible biases. Examine textbooks and materials for gender and cultural bias.*

13) Girls think survival techniques are important to know; boys regard knowledge and how to do things as important to know. The concepts of relationships and taking care of self are major concerns to girls. Historically girls have been taught to connect with others whereas boys have been encouraged to be independent. In this project boys generally believe they are better than girls because they can do more. They also think they know more than girls. Educators need to realize that at this time in their lives middle school boys and girls tend to approach life differently, and therefore what they find necessary to know or believe as they become adults also differs.

Cooperative learning activities are especially important for girls while less important for boys. *Incorporate cooperative learning techniques in classes, encourage girls to try varied activities, expect girls to try new things. Do not let the boys conduct all the experiments and always take the lead. Encourage boys to connect more to others in positive ways and value relationships, and encourage them to express and experience their feelings. Do not let them get in the way of girls' trying things.*

14) What young adolescents do in their free time varies considerably. They study, play music, engage in sports, watch TV, listen to the radio, read, hang out with friends, relax, daydream, draw, sleep, or talk on the phone. The variety of activities they engage in during their own time demonstrates the variety of their personal interests. *Explore what students do in their free time, have them share their interests and hobbies, and provide opportunities for students to explore new activities.* Many young adolescents don't have free time because of a full calendar of activities, but others yearn for interesting things to do.

Try to provide after school activities that might engage students. Too often sports programs, and perhaps music, are the only options offered. Cartooning, T-shirt design, puppetry, safety programs, dance, computer, cooking, and etiquette classes are among proven after school activities.

15) Sleep is important for young adolescents. Sleep should not be viewed as an escape or a sign of laziness, but a way to nurture growing bodies. Simply put, young adolescents need sleep. During sleep the hormones that stimulate growth are produced and utilized. For appropriate physical growth to occur in young adolescents so must sleep.

Middle school educators should discuss the importance of sleep and help young adolescents analyze their schedules and keep a record of their sleep times. Educators should be sensitive to the demands that growth places on young adolescent bodies. It is hard work building a body. While not advocating a nap in class, perhaps an occasional rest period or quiet time would be in order.

16) The concept and practice of play is diminished as fifth and sixth graders mature into seventh and eighth graders. It is important that young adolescents still have opportunites to play. Play provides many benefits – relaxation, creativity, socialization, imagination. It is unfortunate that as youngsters mature they replace the notion of play with more serious and stressful matters. This is of particular concern when we know that adults today have little time to play and often have forgotten how. If more play time is encouraged during the middle school years, young adolescents might feel less stress and develop better lifetime recreational skills as they mature. With more play, less TV might be watched, positive socialization behaviors and friendships would be established, and health and fitness might be improved.

During classes, advisory, and/or exploratories incorporate a spirit of play. Go to a playground, build a snowperson, create art, dance, cook, or play board games. Help students explore the parameters of play and playing.

Study the history of recreation activities in other cultures and during earlier periods of American history. When students learn how children play in other cultures and in other times, they might reassess the place and importance of play in their own lives.

17) Fifth grade girls are more active physically than older girls. This might be attributed to the more mature bodies the older girls are achieving and the transitions they need to make to compete in athletics. Seventh and eighth grade girls' bodies are in their growth peak; they are beginning to feel awkward or think that others believe them to be so. They also are investing a lot of time and energy in making new relationships. *Be sensitive to the physiological and anatomical changes in young adolescents and how these changes might impact participation in physical activities and social relationships. Recommend books to your students that deal with growing up.*

18) Young adolescent boys identify with a variety of celebrated role models, while girls note very few celebrated women as role models. Boys typically chose an athlete as a role model, especially Michael Jordan. Not to burst anyone's bubble, but educators have to help boys realize how rare it is to become a professional athlete. Our girls' bubbles have already been burst. Girls frequently mentioned that they don't have the same athletic career potential as men when asked the biggest difference between the genders. *Recommend books whose characters are good role models. Encourage students to have realistic role models.* Research on the value of role models reveals that they should be visible in the daily lives of young adolescents in order to provide an image of what they can become. Everyday heroes and heroines are the most effective. For example, Mother Hale of the Hale House in New York City has mirrors hung in several places throughout the home so that the young people can see themselves frequently. Through visually accepting themselves they learn to value themselves and see themselves as being special individuals.

19) When wanting to meet someone alive or dead, most young adolescents want to meet a relative, usually a grandfather, who died before they were born. Because young adolescents value their families and their roots so highly, *educators should provide opportunities to study the concept of family* and perhaps give students the opportunity to develop their family stories.

20) Hair is important to young adolescents. The concept of hair has been addressed previously in middle level research and this study affirms how important hair is to middle level students. With so many changes occurring in young adolescents' lives, hair is one of the few things they feel they can control. Hair is a means of creating an individualized image and personality.

Color, length, and style are choices a young adolescent can establish to either conform or make some kind of statement. Young adolescent girls' hair styles are highly influenced by TV, movie stars, and fashion models. Jennifer Aniston (Rachel) from *Friends* created the look that many girls emulate in the mid-1990s as Farrah Fawcett did in the 1970s in *Charlie's Angels*. Boys also care about their hair and often base their styles on athletic trends like the skateboard cut, long on top and shaved underneath. A bad hair day for young adolescents is a serious obstacle for learning. Be sensitive. The frequency one finds students' lockers include a mirror on the inside of the door is a testament to their concern over their appearance.

Provide mirrors in the classroom so students can check themselves out occasionally. Middle school students express a need to go to the bathroom when all they want to do is check themselves out. If mirrors are in a classroom the frequent need to leave class for a vanity-reality check will be decreased. Place the mirror by the waste paper basket and students will clean out back packs and desks so they can catch a peek at themselves, if put by the pencil sharpener you will notice sharper pencils in class.

21) Girls write longer, more detailed responses than boys. Their lengthier responses might be attributed to girls' experience writing in diaries or because they haven't been able to participate equally in class discussions, or just because of a greater need to express themselves. Girls need the opportunity to speak in class and the encouragement to do so. *Use wait time, recognize students who have raised their hands rather than accepting answers of students who call out. Employ a technique that ensures all students will get called on and recognized.* One example: give students the same number of Skittles at the start of class. Once a student has spoken he/she gets to eat a Skittle. When the students' three or four Skittles are gone they can't speak anymore. Students love this technique, it works, it teaches a lesson, and provides the confidence that some students need.

Encourage boys to write more poems, reflective pieces, and lyrics to songs. Boys need to feel more comfortable with intrapersonal expression. Some boys have little trouble writing about what they think and feel, others are at a loss. Play different kinds of music and ask students what they think the meanings of the songs are; show a clip of a movie or TV show and ask students what the clip has to do with their lives. It's not important whether students write lengthy or short responses, rather that they have opportunities to think, reflect on their thinking, and build confidence in their abilities to express themselves.

22) Trust is important to young adolescents. They want to trust themselves, their friends, their teachers, and their families. For young adolescents to be trusted is a hallmark of becoming more mature. *School policies relating to restroom passes and hallway behavior should demonstrate trust in students rather than reflect distrust or create a prison-like atmosphere.* Young adolescents must experience a trusting environment with trustworthy people. They need to feel capable of being a part of a trusting environment.

23) Young adolescents want to communicate. They would like to communicate more honestly with friends, families, and society. Somehow early in life children seem to learn not to share their thoughts and feelings, maybe because they think that what they think may be stupid, or maybe because they were told that "children should be seen and not heard."

The need for young adolescents to gain confidence in communicating was very apparent in *Hostile Hallways* (1993). The research revealed that students do not usually report harassment incidents to adults, and that girls are twice as likely to report them as boys (p. 14). The study cites that less than 7 percent of sexually harassed students have told a teacher, and fewer than one in four (23%) have told a parent or other family member, and that 77 percent of girls and 49 percent of boys have told their friends (p. 24). *Model positive communication skills. Provide opportunities for students to communicate with each other, relatives, or teachers through letter writing, or E-mail messages, and interviews with a variety of people. Share results. Write scripts for radio, TV, or newscasts. Prepare excerpts of TV shows on critical issues and have the students discuss their thoughts about them. Go to senior citizens' homes to interview individuals about their lives as children.* Provide a nonthreatening supportive way for young adolescents to realize that you care about their concerns and worries. When we least expect it a young adolescent may come to us and reveal a serious concern. We should be prepared to listen without being judgmental.

24) Young adolescents did not connect the concept of language to how words impact people. Young adolescents recognize how painful words are and want their friends, families, and teachers to be more sensitive to their feelings and to those of other kids. Physical fights receive immediate attention from educators, but the scars from verbal harassment are seldom treated. *Be careful how you use words and how you monitor their use by others.* Let students know you will not tolerate put-downs, name calling, or abusive language. *Help them to recognize the emotional side of language.*

25) Young adolescents have not developed an adult concept of time. Middle school students do not have a clear vision of past life events and where they fit into the time line of history. According to 10-14 year olds, World War II and even Vietnam are ancient history, while hair spray and penicillin are inventions within their lifetime. Since many young adolescents have not yet developed abstract cognitive ability and still function on the concrete level, it is not surprising that students' "least favorite class" is often social studies. *Regardless of class content (history, literature, art , core, encore) utilize the concept of reverse chronology. Have students create a time line of events in their* *lives and then travel backwards, rather than traveling from the past toward the present.* Once young adolescents have connected events that happened during their lifetime, then connecting to the past becomes more comfortable for them.

26) Pets are important to young adolescents. Students enjoy talking about their pets and sharing pet stories. Pets bring great joy to young adolescents as well as teach responsibility. Young adolescents' ownership of pets extends past cats and dogs. Occasionally a student in class will unexpectedly share that his or her pet has recently died or experienced an injury. Pet stories provide a range of emotions and outlets of laughter and tears. *Provide opportunities for students to talk about their pets. Have a pet show and a pet day when students can bring pets to school, and/or write pet stories and poems.*

27) Young adolescents focus on God and Jesus in a variety of responses. Many young adolescents have strong religious beliefs. Their faiths provide a value base and role models. A majority of the students did not voice any religious beliefs, but for those that did it was important. *Recognize the beliefs of some students but do not expect that all students have similar beliefs and faiths, although they might have some form of spirituality.*

28) Young adolescents are avid media consumers. Never before has there been such a need for a media literacy curriculum. Television, print ads, music, and commercials are prominent in the social realities of all young adolescents. Their appearance, wants, desires, and interests are greatly influenced by media exposure. Young adolescents' identity is often measured by what they see in the media. Middle level students need guidance in becoming informed media consumers. Educators and parents alike need to teach students how to become critical consumers and recognize that much of what is depicted in the media is unrealistic.

Utilize various media in your classes. Their interests in media scopes from music, magazines, TV and movies, to videos. John Davies' (1996) *Educating Students in a Media-Saturated Culture,* is an excellent resource for studying the mass media culture of students. His suggestions for a media literacy curriculum are readily applicable to the classroom.

Music becomes a signature of personality during this period of life. Young adolescent images and identities are often based on the fads and fashions of musical groups. MTV is very exciting for many 10-15 year olds. What is important for educators to address about MTV are the hidden and overt messages delivered: how men and women are perceived; their sexual fantasies and sexual behaviors, and the violence inherent in the words and actions. Educators know that young adolescents function at different levels of cognitive thinking, therefore some middle school students may not be able to separate reality, truth, and fantasies in the messages they receive from music videos and television shows. Teachers can help them critique such messages. *Ask students to bring in their favorite music, have them study the history behind the music, the band, and analyze the message and poetry of the lyrics. Allowing them to explore and research their music culture promotes validation of their interests and culture.*

There are many ways to include music in your curriculum, regardless of course content. Sevn resources to help young adolescents become media literate follow:

1) Parent Music Research Center, 1500 Arlington Blvd. Suite 300, Arlington, VA 22209. A good resource for music and song lyrics. The organization provides school and family resource books. This organization is responsible for coding music labels for parents regarding lyrics of songs.

2) Foundation for Media Education, Sut Jhalley. (413) 586-8398. 26 Center Street, Northhampton, MA. 01060. *Dreamworlds 1, Dreamworlds 2* are very interesting videos that explain the strategies, impact, and implications of MTV. *Pack of Lies: The Advertizing of Tobacco* is a video that describes the implication and strategies of tobacco advertising. Powerful portrayal of implied media messages.

3) *Still Killing Them Softly*, Jean Kilbourne (617) 354-3677. Cambridge Documentary Films, P.O. Box 386 Cambridge, MA. 02139. An excellent discourse of the overt and covert messages in advertising is the video. The video describes the implication and strategies of advertising.

4) *Gender Advertisement,* Goffman, E. (1979) Cambridge, MA: Harvard University Press.

5) *Captive Kids,* (1995) a report on commercial pressures on kids at school, prepared by Zillions; For kids. from *Consumer Reports.*

6) *Extra, The Magazine of Fair.* 130 West 25th Street, New York, NY 10001. (212) 663-6700.

7) *Educating Students in a Media-Saturated Cuture,* John Davies (1996). Lancaster, PA: Technomic (800) 233-9936.

As you help your students become media literate also encourage them to become media activists regarding their media concerns and interests. Guide them in their communications to television and radio stations, and newspapers and magazines with the following list of addresses and telephone numbers.

NETWORK TELEVISION

ABC News
47 W. 66 St.
New York, NY 10023
Phone: (212) 456-7777
FAX: (212) 456-4968
DC Bureau
Phone: (202) 222-7777

ABC World News Tonight
Phone: (212) 456-4040

Nightline
Phone: (202) 222-7000

Prime Time Live
Phone: (212) 456-1200

20/20
Phone: (212) 456-2020

CBS News
524 W. 57th St.
New York, NY 10019
Phone: (212) 975-4321
FAX (212) 975-1893
D.C. Bureau
Phone: (202) 457-4321

CBS Evening News
Phone: (212) 975-3691

CBS This Morning
Phone: (212) 975-2824

60 Minutes
Phone: (212) 975-2009

CNN
1 CNN Center
Box 105366
Atlanta, GA 30348-5366
Phone: (404) 827-1500
FAX: (404) 827-1593
820 First St. N.E.
Washington, DC 20002
Phone: (202) 898-7900
FAX: (202) 898-7923

Crossfire
Phone: (202) 898-7655

Larry King Live
Phone: (202) 898-7690

NBC News
30 Rockefeller Plaza
New York, NY 10112
Phone: (212) 664-4444
FAX: (212) 664-5705
D.C. Bureau
Phone: (202) 885-4200

NBC Nightly News
Phone: (212) 664-4971

Today
Phone: (212) 664-4249

PUBLIC BROADCASTING

PBS
1320 Braddock Place
Alexandria, VA 22314
Phone: (703) 739-5000
FAX: (703) 739-0775

National Public Radio
635 Massachusetts Ave. N.W.
Washington, DC 20001-3753
Phone: (202) 414-2000
FAX: (202) 414-3329

McNeil/Lehrer NewsHour
356 W. 58th St.
New York, NY 10019
Phone: (212) 560-3113
FAX: (212) 560-3117

All Things Considered
Phone: (202) 414-2110

Morning Edition
Phone: (202) 414-2150

NATIONAL NEWSPAPERS

Los Angeles Times
Time-Mirror Square
Los Angeles, CA 90053
Phone: (800) 528-4637
FAX: (213) 237-4712

Wall Street Journal
200 Liberty Street
New York, NY 10281
Phone: (212) 416-2000
FAX: (212) 416-2658

New York Times
229 W. 43rd St.
New York, NY 10036
Phone: (212) 556-1234
FAX: (212) 556-3690
D.C. Bureau
Phone: (202) 862-0300

Washington Post
1150 15th St. N.W.
Washington, DC 20071
Phone: (202) 334-6000
FAX: (202) 334-5451

USA Today
1000 Wilson Blvd.
Arlington, VA 22229
Phone: (800) 828-0909
FAX: (703) 276-5513

Associated Press
50 Rockefeller Plaza
New York, NY 10020
National Desk:
(212) 621-1600
Foreign Desk:
(212) 621-1663
D.C. Bureau:
(202) 828-6400

MAGAZINES

Newsweek
251 W. 57th St.
New York, NY 10019
Phone: (212) 445-4000
FAX: (212) 445-5068

U.S. News & World Report
2400 N. St. N.W.
Washington, DC 20037
Phone: (202) 955-2000
FAX: (202) 955-2049

Time
Time, Inc.
Time & Life Bldg.
Rockefeller Center
New York, NY 10020
Phone: (212) 522-1212
FAX (212) 522-0323

Magazines provide an endless supply of "how to's," "what to's" and "what's in" directed at young adolescents. They become the directions on how to be a contemporary adolescent, especially for girls. Girls enjoy reading *Seventeen, Sassy,* and *YM.* Boys' magazines focus more on sports, computers, and music than on appearance. However, *Playboy* is a favorite magazine of some young adolescent boys. *Go to magazine racks and note the types of magazines; observe what young adolescents chose to purchase or stand by and read. Consider having students study advertisements and the range of articles, then reach some conclusions on the value, strengths, and weaknesses of the magazines.*

A recent activity I did with a seventh grade advisory class was a research project based on *Seventeen* magazine. We spent a week on this project (could have used at least two weeks). Each student had his/her own copy of the magazine. The first day we examined the cover of the magazine – the type of photograph, men and/or women, on the cover (then we graphed gender and composition of front covers) and studied the words. Then the students were asked to respond to the question, Why would anyone buy this magazine based on the cover? We spent the next two days exploring size and composition of advertisements and the messages being provided. The fourth day we examined the content of the feature articles to see the article contents and implications of what this magazine represents, and on the final day we examined *MS Magazine.* (*MS* carries no advertisements.) We compared the appearance and content of the two magazines. A variety of interesting conclusions were reached. You can imagine some of the comments.

Such a project provides a rich integration of curricula. Obviously, any magazine could be used for this activity, and you and your students would develop your own approach. But this activity that involves both content and process also directly ties to the young adolescent culture.

Young adolescents' tastes in television shows tend to be similar. They enjoy family situation comedies the most. As they reach eighth grade boys may watch detective and FBI shows more. The boys like science fiction and adventure movies and TV more than girls. In addition to the situation comedies girls like *90210* and *ER*.

Explore the different types of TV shows, movies, and commercials that your students watch. Have them research their favorite shows and movies. Initiate discussions during which students can express their thoughts, reflect on issues raised, and formulate new understandings.

Three organizations that can help teach about television literacy are:

1) *Teaching Around Television,* The New Mexico Media Literacy Project. Albuquerque Academy, 6400 Wyoming Boulevard, NE Albuquerque, New Mexico, 87109. (505) 828-3264 sponsored by the state to make New Mexico the first media literate state.

2) National Coalition on Television Violence, Box 2157, Champagne, IL 61825. Committed to decreasing the violence in films and television.

3) Center for Media Education, 1511 K. Street, NW Suite 518, Washington, DC. 20005 (202) 628-2620. A pioneer organization trying to improve children's television.

29) Young adolescents strongly favor family situation comedies. When viewing such shows young adolescents act as peeping Toms, examining how other families are dealing with some of the same contemporary issues their family may be experiencing. *Take a poll of favorite shows and have students do a variety of research projects based on their polls. Lead discussions concerning what makes certain shows favorites.*

Young adolescents still enjoy watching cartoons. Some are family cartoons such as *Simpsons* and *Bobbie's World*. It is fun for young adolescents to transcend their in-between age through the media of cartoons. Take time out some Saturday morning or after school and watch these cartoons. You may be in for a pleasant surprise.

Young Adolescents' Perceptions of Family

1) Young adolescents worry about family members, disease, death, divorce, violence, and the condition of the earth. Students want to discuss the many things going on daily that they see on TV. Magic Johnson's return to basketball after retiring because he has the HIV virus, the capture of the alleged unabomber, the Atlanta Olympic bombing, the Nicole Simpson Brown and Ron Goldman murders, first amendment rights, or the controversy over teaching evolution are events that students seek help in understanding. They provide relevant "teachable moments."

Provide ongoing opportunities for students to discuss their concerns. When faced with devastating situations in their lives, young adolescents need a time to articulate and construct their moral reasoning. In class dialogues students are given supportive and nurturing opportunities to express their thoughts and clarify their views. Young adolescents want to share these worries with their families, but on their terms. And these needs can only be addressed when they are ready but not because they have to have things their way.

As teachers we should not expect just to ask students what worries them and expect a fluent conversation. We need to provide a nonthreatening, supportive climate in which young adolescents are comfortable expressing their concerns and worries. Parents should also try to provide such an atmosphere.

Create a forum for dialogue with teachers, educational leaders, and parents. In such forums answers are not sought so much simply providing opportunities for adults to share their thoughts on local or world events and what influence these events might have on students. Viewpoints from different groups open communication that might enhance parent involvement as well as provide a meaningful and successful educational experience for all. These forums assist parents with parenting skills and create opportunities for parents to dialogue with young adolescents on family relationships and appropriate restrictions.

2) Young adolescents enjoy being with their families. Schools can help young adolescents and their families spend time together by providing activities through the school that parents can participate in such as ski trips, picnics, movie nights, community service projects, picnics, and potluck meals. An occasional evening when the media center, computer lab, gym, and other facilities are open and all are invited for informal activities, games, or just "hanging around" will bring many family members and their children to school. Family involvement in schools benefits the school, child, family, and community. *Create a family-friendly environment where adults and students feel welcomed and wanted.*

3) Mothers are more influential in the lives of young adolescents than fathers. This may be the result of the number of single parent families or the greater role that mothers traditionally play in the lives of children. Whatever the reason, the reduced role of fathers is a concern. *Be sensitive to how mothers and fathers are discussed and portrayed in the curriculum, in comments, and in school functions and publications.* Diverse family compositions may not fit some traditional functions like father-son, or mother-daughter activities. Avoid functions that separate activities by gender. Rather have a family and friends banquet. Many young adolescents today may only have or have access to one parent, or may not have either parent. Also avoid making mothers' and fathers' day cards and gifts. These activities really do not belong in the classroom and interfere with the self-esteem of some children.

4) Young adolescents want to tell their families that they love them, but... Although they want to share both positive and negative thoughts and experiences with their parents, they feel uncomfortable doing so. The problem may be more in the inability of the adults to set the proper stage than it is in the reticence of young adolescents to speak out. *Help parents develop communication skills with their young adolescents through workshops, newsletter tips, and student-led conferences.*

5)   Young adolescents dislike their siblings. Teachers may feel they are complimenting students by comparing them to siblings, but most students dislike such comparisons *Avoid comparing siblings to each other and view each young adolescent as an individual who has his/her own unique interests and abilities.* Young adolescents are in the process of learning who they are, creating their own identity. They want recognition for their uniqueness. Honor those things that make every child special.

Young Adolescents' Perceptions of School

1)   Grades are a major concern for young adolescents. Although the elimination of competitive grades is not immediately achievable, educators should work to provide other more valid ways of assessing progress including opportunities for self-evaluation and the demonstration of skills learned. *Portfolio assessments and student led conferences provide a more holistic and accurate assessment of one's own performance.*

Since tests and grades are stressful to young adolescents and impact their self-concepts, methods of evaluation should be success oriented and less judgmental. Assessment measures should not compare one student with another, rather compare one's previous status with current status. With so much developmental and experiential variance among young adolescents, it makes little sense to compare one adolescent to another. Written tests are not always the best assessment tool for all students. Some do better on oral examinations. Try to include activities and assessments that recognize several types of intelligence.

2) Young adolescents do not like or appreciate homework, especially if it is not relevant. Make an effort to assign homework that is understood, recognized as related to class goals, and not readily categorized as busywork. Homework to be turned in should be read and evaluated by the teacher and returned in a timely fashion lest students start to believe that the assignments are not important or valued. If teachers expect students to value homework assignments, so must the teachers.

The importance of academics is not in question, but when

students have three hours of homework nightly, somehow priorities have to be questioned. As some of the students wrote, "We're only kids once."

It is important for teachers and parents to appreciate that the workload tolerance is different in children than in adults and can vary from child to child. After returning home from class one night, a student of mine found this letter her seventh grade child had written as if he were the parent. In a young adolescent voice the need for teaming, advisory, and decreased homework is vigorously illustrated.

Dear Ms. _____,

I am an extremely concerned mother of a student of yours. My child constantly complains about how much homework he receives. I have talked about the amount he receives over with other concerned mothers and they all agree that it is child abuse. I am not pinpointing the main source of homework on you, that is without doubt math, but as you know I am not able to contact Mrs.____ at the moment.

I have also noticed that you give homework to the children on weekends. That is just ridiculous! You probably think that since the kids have two days off of school they have more time to do homework. My child and many others spend three to four hours on homework every night when they already spend seven and a half hours at school! The weekend is supposed to be two days of fun for them. But they only rest because they are so tired from staying up late every day because of homework! Plus they have to do more homework on the week end! Where does it stop? It is getting sickening. My child has gotten ill because of his tired state.

When you were a child didn't you have fun or free time? Kids have to have fun besides doing work. My kid often gets extremely frustrated with homework and begins crying and tearing papers and kicking chairs and tables over while screaming about how he can't take any more work. He even sometimes says he wishes that he could quit school. He always complains that the work ruins his life. He comes home and sleeps from exhaustion and then gets up and does homework for way too long. Many of the conversations we have concern his hate for school. At home he is now always in a bad mood and cranky from too much work and tiredness. He spends an hour-and-a-half on math alone! It is rare when he gets a week-end without homework. He has never had a single week day without homework. Math every single day is just disgusting. And they get tons of math too. Can't they prove they know how to do a type of a math problem in twenty problems instead of three pages of it?

It does ruin my child's life. He never has any fun any-more. I know that seventh grade is planned harder than sixth or eighth grade, but this is a nightmare. Along the line of nightmares, my kid has nightmares about going to school and getting another project assigned. The im-pact paper you recently assigned is horrible! A two or three page hand written paper due the next day! Along with other work! Well, there goes my kid's day. Also, they had to do the European Trip while reading two novels and do reports on them both! My child was ready to col-lapse! Which he did. Do you teachers want all your stu-dents to develop ulcers? Well, that's what all this is lead-ing to. I could go on for ever, but I don't have the time.

Please take this letter seriously. I would really appre-ciate you showing this letter to other teachers. Try to make a change. If you really are a good teacher you will. Please.

Sincerely,
A concerned mother

The young adolescent student who wrote this letter felt he had legitimate complaints. Several times in my graduate class his mother had discussed her concerns about his homework situation. She had previously talked with his teachers about her concerns. Although she was aware of the situation, this letter came to her as a surprise.

Provide students and parents a syllabus and team calendar of events with project due dates and test dates so that students, with family support, can budget time for homework, school, so-cial, and family activities. This will help students plan ahead and organize. What may seem like a little work to an individual teacher may seem overwhelming to a young adolescent, especially when added to other assignments given by other teachers, home responsibilities, and school or community related activities.

Reduce or eliminate worksheets, especially prepackaged ones. Students now start getting worksheets in preschool and kindergarten, so by the time they reach middle school, worksheets have little attraction to the expanding minds of young adolescents.

3) Young adolescents have a strong sense of fairness. Their perception of fairness is explained by Gilligan and associates (1991) in their research on the moral development of girls. This work demonstrated that justice is important to the girls as Kohlberg's work (1984) demonstrated that the determination of right from wrong is important to boys. *Appreciate the possible differences in how boys and girls approach moral dilemmas.* Regardless of how middle school students execute their moral dilemmas they expect teachers to be fair and just, not to be partial or play favorites.

4) Young adolescents do not understand what principals really do. Students see principals as being in charge of the school, but they are uncertain what the job entails. They want their principals to be more visible. *Principals should be actively involved in classes whenever possible and not just pop in. Students want principals to check up on teachers more frequently and hire better substitutes.*

5) Fifth and eighth graders perceive differently the qualities of a good student. Perceptions about the qualities of a good student alter as they mature. Initially good grades and good behavior are important to younger students. The eighth graders, having experienced a couple of years of middle school, realize that a good student is friendly and exhibits positive behaviors. They realize too that although making good grades is important, grades alone do not comprise a good student. *Discuss with your students the attributes of a good student.* A common vision of desirable student attributes will result and become a recognized goal.

6) Middle school kids listen to inner voices. Young adolescents put on internal tapes in their minds and play them over and over: "Why are you so clumsy?" "Can't you do anything right?" "Why can't you get organized?" "How many times do I have to tell you? "How can you be so stupid?" Young adolescents hear such phrases time after time from parents, friends, and sometimes even from teachers, and they internalize them.

Be careful how language is used and be sensitive to how words contribute to the overt loss of voice in students, and to the internal voices that young adolescents play regularly in their minds. Young adolescents are encouraged to like themselves, but these assertions must be backed up with opportunities for them to experience success, not be subjected to negative verbal messages.

7) Young adolescents want to discuss school with their families. Students would welcome a forum to discuss their school concerns with their families. *Student-led conferences are a great way for students to discuss with their families their progress in achievement and related school issues in a safe environment.* The process allows both students and parent to discuss and share educational issues in a constructive, responsible method that could transfer to home discussions.

General Invitations

1) Take the initiative and involve students in sharing concerns and thoughts. Become an inquirer. Build connections between you and your students to open doorways of thought and curriculum possibilities that cannot be provided by a packaged program or textbook. At first make the inquiry informal. Young adolescents may not have confidence in expressing their thoughts; they need time to become comfortable sharing them. Stevenson's books *Teachers as Inquirers: Srategies for Teaching With and About Early Adolescents* (1986), and *Teaching 10-14 Year Olds* (1992), and *The Inquiry Process, Student-Centered Learning*, by Ross M. Burkhardt (1994) are excellent sources of suggestions and guidelines on ways to become inquirers. You can use the statementaire from this project or have students create an instrument for gathering their thoughts and ideas.

Finding student voice is more than an interesting experience, but reaching out to students' thoughts does not mean that you are becoming a counselor or therapist. This is not a touchy-feely activity, although some teachers might choose to embrace such a notion. When students express and share their thoughts in their own voices teachers have the opportunity to recognize students as intelligent beings and not as receptacles in which to store others' thoughts and canned information. Students bring with them an abundance of experiences that shape and form their beliefs and attitudes, and educators should build on these experiences.

Students want to learn. They like to think and to construct concepts and ideas. In this study students often responded that the best thing about school was learning something new and that they enjoy active experiences, especially when they are shared with others. But isolated in school year after year, saddled to textbooks and worksheets, students' interest in learning wanes and school becomes merely an exercise of putting in time and filling in spaces. This is not education, at best it is training.

Develop confidence in your own thoughts and in connecting them to the students' thoughts.

2) Design ways to include your school's leadership team as an integral part of your classes. Invite your administrative leaders to come into the classroom, get them actively engaged with students. Also have students interview and work with principals on various projects. Even though they are indeed busy, principals like to be included in learning activities.

3) Create an exploratory class or a day in the advisory program based on student thoughts. Current events, both locally and nationally, music, media, and the things going on in school are sources for discussions. Events go on daily that students see on TV or hear about. They need a chance to discuss them. When faced with so many moral dilemmas and tragic situations in real life, young adolescents need a time to "think out loud" and refine their moral reasoning. In class dialogues students should have the opportunity to express their thoughts and clarify their views under the guidance of a trusted adult.

4) Create a forum for teachers and educational leaders to dialogue with parents and other adults. Expressions of thought from different persons or groups opens communications that will expand parent and community involvement as well as provide meaningful educational experiences for the participants. These should not be gripe sessions, but dialogues on and about what young adolescents think, what they are doing, and how school programs address their needs.

5) Create a family-friendly, community-friendly school. Involve parents in meaningful ways. Parents have diverse knowledge, experiences, and vocations. Yet their vast and varied knowledge, for the most part, is seldom tapped by the schools. The same is true with other community citizens. When schools establish an inviting climate and offer various activities in which adults can participate, the morale of the school increases and its reputation improves.

Positive feelings about the school may be held by those adults involved in sports, band, or other special programs. But what about the families of those young adolescents who are not tied to those programs? Can they feel inclusionary pride? Consider ways to involve persons with intersts in art, science, literature, or other areas.

6) Never before has it been so important for educators and the students themselves to realize their full potential. Violence and crime are common strands in the lives of many young adolescents. Such behaviors ripple and sometimes thunder through schools and communities. Educators have the opportunity and responsibility to provide a safe, nurturing environment that promotes success for each student and counters the violence prevalent outside of school. Historically schools have provided success for those students who fit within certain expectations and patterns. This perception has to change. Educators need to become active promoters of success and self-actualization, helping all students find their own personal identity and brilliance. This can be assisted by providing opportunities to listen to and be influenced by student voices. By incorporating student conversations, teachers will begin to make the needed paradigm shift. In order to fulfill the new role of coach, facilitator, or director of learning that is called for in curriculum integration efforts, teachers have to reconsider and expand their self-concepts. Over time, the narrow role of instructor in a single subject has likely diminished one's self-concept.

7) Create mentor programs. Schools should initiate "shadow days" during which students can enter the community to shadow individuals and experience different career possibilities. These days are sandwiched between class activities that provide appropriate background knowledge, preparation, and follow-up discussions. Two or three career shadow days a year beginning in sixth grade would permit young adolescents to sample different fields of work and begin to relate educational experiences to some of their career visions. Shadow activities create positive school, family, and community relations in addition to helping young adolescents connect to their communities and possible careers. Local branches of the American Association of University Women are excellent sources for shadowing. This organization seeks opportunities to provide young adolescents with rich opportunities. Community service organizations such as Kiwanis, Lions, and Rotary are also good resources.

8) Create a "rites of passage" curriculum. Design special and distinctive activities for each grade level. Lacking positive school activities to look forward to as they mature kids may possibly engage in inappropriate and unacceptable behaviors. If each grade level had a special rite of passage activity for students to anticipate, then possibly other questionable behaviors will be put on hold and/or eliminated. Special activities could include an overnight camping trip, a continuing experience with a challenging rope course, an overnight community service, or involvement in a Habitat for Humanity house building. Rites of passage curricula need to be challenging to excite students and build their self-esteem. A certain degree of risk taking and the mastering of new skills is involved, making the activity one they may look forward to with almost as much enthusiasm as getting a driver's license.

9) Have students create personal 'zines to define and explore themselves and their young adolescent culture. 'Zines are like underground newspapers in which individuals write about themselves and their interests. The word 'zine comes from magazine. So, a 'zine can resemble a very modest magazine. Students enjoy creating them. They can work in small groups or by themselves. They can cut out magazine pictures that represent what's important to them; write lyrics to songs or create poems; take school surveys about music, food, or interests; or follow their ideas wherever they take them. This project provides an opportunity for students to clarify their interests and create a project that allows them to share their culture in a personalized way. 'Zines also provide you a vehicle to discover young adolescent culture through their eyes.

10) Create a peace curriculum. If war is to be studied in the curriculum then so too should be peace. Frequently social studies classes study history from a war-to-war perspective without acknowledging the power of peace and the role of peacemakers. Study peacemakers like Pilgrim Peace, the Quakers, and Martin Luther King, Jr. If we provide alternatives to the study of war in our social studies and language arts curricula, maybe a generation of peacemakers will result.

11) Create a humor curriculum and include humor in your life and in the lives of young adolescents. The positive effect laughter has on us through the different endorphins that the brain releases is well known. Endorphins are a substance whose molecular substance is similar to morphine and are the body's own way of relaxing and relieving pain The effect of laughter on the body is commonly recognized. Remember that great feeling when you get the giggles? Or how much your sides or belly might hurt from laughter? Something good is happening to us when we laugh.

Young adolescent lives are complicated and stressful. Lacking the skills needed to make themselves and others feel good, they may make fun of others. Albert Schweitzer wrote of humor as a way of reducing one's temperature and tensions; Imanuel Kant tells us that laughter produces a feeling of health, and Sir William Osler viewed laughter as the "music of life." As music is important to young adolescents, so is humor.

Have a "humor day" in class where non-racist, non-sexist, age appropriate jokes or riddles are shared. At the end of a quiz give extra points for including an appropriate joke. It's fun for students and a great way to make scoring the quizzes more enjoyable . Have students post comic strips on bulletin boards or create their own comic strips. TV situation comedies and cartoon shows can be analyzed for their comic impact.

If educators are too serious, as studies suggest, they will benefit from a humor curriculum. If we can help ourselves and our students release these endorphins and laugh more, society might "lighten up" too.

12) **Respond to the questions your students ask and to their suggestions.** Even the most bizarre questions or ideas deserve explanation or consideration. Creative thoughts often lead to new discoveries and inventions. Although something may not seem important to you, it may be very important to the student. Nick, an eighth grade student, once wrote me:

> ... schools raise kids to be conformists, by having a curriculum that teaches everyone the same unimportant things about the same time. When it comes time for us to go to high school and we are asked 'What do you want to learn?' We don't know, because we have been forced fed the same worthless information and have been given no opportunities to expand upon personal talents, the only 'real' thing that will make us 'productive members of society.' The people in the history books who are called geniuses and are considered as having great minds were usually people who were 'different' and thought new and exciting things that were repressed by the school system that now revenge them while smothering the growth of brilliant young minds.

Explicit thinking for an eighth grade student.

13) **Never ask students a question you know the answer to.** Why should we ask questions when the answers are known? Encourage students to think beyond the obvious. It is important for teachers and students to think past the known and explore and create the unknown. This process allows students to construct knowledge and use their imagination. It also allows us avenues to explore and understand different thoughts (re-read Nick's letter).

14) **Create opportunities for young adolescents to become politically active.** To develop an interest and knowledge of how society works students need to become politically active and proactive with societal issues. They have broadening interests and seek more knowledge. If educators infuse their curriculum with contemporary issues, education becomes meaningful. Young adolescents have serious concerns about the environment, ecology, poverty, war, homelessness, and hunger. They want to make a difference. If students are given the opportunity to write letters or E-mail the President or their congressional representatives they will develop a politically active voice that might stay active as they become adults.

Letters written to the local newspaper or advertisers on television shows provide another avenue for a political voice. Let students study an issue that individually concerns them and write an appropriate letter. Every class member does not have to support the same cause. As diverse as students are, so are the issues they want to advocate. Students can learn to express their individual perspective as young adolescents and find the confidence that comes with expressing their voice. Schools can have Community Service Fairs where students display their work and talk with people about the actions they took. Grassroots programs through schools have lasting effects on the students.

15) Create a media literacy curriculum in your team. To help them better understand the media and the hidden messages found in media, a serious study of media is a most appropriate part of the curriculum.

Your Thoughts

While reading this monograph you have had many thoughts, and possibly some new ideas popped into your head. How can they be incorporated into your teaching? One step any teacher can take is to create a classroom environment that is a safe haven for you and your students. Be the teacher who fully shares the "jar of marbles." Better yet, let the students bring in their own jars of whatever they want to share, and you and the class investigate and learn together. The advice that Dewey offered in 1938 needs to be embraced and practiced today more than ever.

Experience does not go on simply inside a person. It does go on there for it influences the formations of desires and purpose. But this is not the whole story. Every genuine experience has an active side which changes in some degree the objective conditions under which experiences are had....We live from birth to death in a world of persons and things which in large measure is what it is because of what has been done and transmitted from previous activities. When this fact is ignored, experience is treated as if it were something which goes on exclusively inside an individual's body and mind. It ought not be necessary to say that experience does not occur in a vacuum... There are sources out-

side an individual which give rise to experience.... When their educational import is recognized, they indicate a second way in which an educator can direct experiences of the young without engaging in imposition. Above all they should know how to utilize the surroundings physical and social that exist so as to extract from them all that they have to contribute to building experience worthwhile. (pp. 39-40)

Explore your students' thoughts and social realities. Let them guide you. We cannot wait another 60 years to make education authentic and relevant to the experiences, lives, thoughts, voices, and social realities of our young adolescents. We need to start today. Enjoy. **v**

Recommended Reading

Alicea, C., & DeSena, C. (1995). *The air down there, true tales from a South Bronx boyhood.* San Francisco: Chronicle Books.

American Association of University Women. (1992). *How schools shortchange girls.* AAUW Educational Foundation, Wellesley College.

American Association of University Women. (1993). *Hostile hallways, The AAUW survey on sexual harassment in America's schools.* Washington, DC: AAUW.

American Association of University Women. (1995). *Growing smart: What's working for girls in school.* Washington, DC. AAUW Educational Foundation.

American Association of University Women, (1995). *Growing smart, What's working for girls in school. Executive summary and action guide.* Washington, DC: AAUW Educational Foundation.

Beane, J. & Lipka, R. (1987). *When the kids come first: Enhancing self-esteem.* Columbus, OH: National Middle School Association.

Beane, J. (1993). *A Middle school curriculum: From rhetoric to reality.* (2nd ed.) Columbus, OH: National Middle School Association.

Belenky, M., Lyons, N., Clinchy, B.M., Goldberger, N. R., & Tarule, J. M. (1986). *Women's ways of knowing: The development of self, voice, and mind.* New York: Basic Books.

Bingham, M., Emondson, J., & Stryker, S. (1985). *Challenges: A young man's journal for self-awareness and personal planning.* Santa Barbara, CA: Advocacy Press.

Bingham, M., & Stryker, S. (1995). *Things will be different for my daughter: A practical guide to building her self-esteem and self-reliance.* New York: Penguin Books.

Burkhardt, R. M. (1994). *The inquiry process, Student-centered learning.* Logan, IA: Perfection Learning Corporation.

Carlip, H. (1995). *Girl power, young women speak out!* New York: Warner Books.

Consumers Union Education Services. (1995). *Captive kids: Commercial pressures on kids at school.* New York: Consumers Union Education Services.

Fertman, C., White, G., & White, L (1996). *Service learning in the middle school: Building a culture of service.* Columbus, OH: National Middle School Association.

Gilligan, C., Lyons, N., & Hanmer, T. (1990). *Making connections: The relational worlds of adolescent girls at Emma Willard School.* Cambridge: MA: Harvard University Press.

Gilligan, C., & Brown, L. (1992). *Meeting at the crossroads: The landmark book about the turning points in girls' and women's lives.* New York: Ballantine.

Kennedy, P. (1995). *'Zine.' How I spent six years of my life in the underground and finally...found myself...I think.* New York: St. Martine's Griffin.

Ministry of Education. (1989). *Media literacy: Resource guide.* Ontario, Canada: Ministry of Education.

National Middle School Association. (1995). *This we believe: Developmentally responsive middle level schools.* Columbus, OH: Author.

Oreinstein, P. (1994). *SchoolGirls: Young women, self-esteem, and the confidence gap.* New York: Doubleday.

Pipher, M. (1994). *Reviving Ophelia: Saving the lives of adolescent girls.* New York: Ballatine.

Riley, L., Baldus, R., Belson, O., Schuler, B., & Keyes, M. (1993). *"My worst nightmare." Wisconsin students' perceptions of being the other gender.* Menomonie, WI: University Wisconsin-Stout.

Stevenson, C. (1986). *Teachers as inquirers: Strategies for learning with and about early adolescents.* Columbus, OH: National Middle School Association.

References

Adler, J. (1992, February 17). Hey, I'm terrific. *Newsweek, 119* (7). 46-51.

American Association of University Women. (1992). *The AAUW report: How schools shortchange girls.* Wellesley College: AAUW Educational Foundation.

American Association of University Women. (1993). *Hostile hallways: The AAUW survey on sexual harassment in America's schools.* Washington, DC: Author.

American Association of University Women. (1995). *Growing smart: What's working for girls in school.* Washington, DC: AAUW Educational Foundation.

American Association of University Women. (1995). *Growing smart: What's working for girls in school. Executive summary and action guide.* Washington, DC: AAUW Education Foundation.

Beane, J., & Lipka, R. (1987). *When the kids come first: Enhancing self-esteem.* Columbus, OH: National Middle School Association.

Beane, J. (1993). *A middle school curriculum: From rhetoric to reality* (2nd. ed.). Columbus, OH: National Middle School Association.

Belenky, M., Lyons, N., Clinchy, B.M., Goldberger, N. R., & Tarule, J. M. (1986). *Women's ways of knowing: The development of self, voice, and mind.* New York: Basic Books.

Brodkey, L. (1987). Writing ethnographic narrative. *Written communication, 4,* 25-50.

Burkhardt, R. M. (1994). *The inquiry process, Student-centered learning.* Logan, IA: Perfection Learning Corporation.

Carlip, H. (1995). *Girl power: Young women speak out.* New York: Warner Books.

Consumers Union Education Services. (1995). *Captive kids: Commercial pressures on kids at school.* New York: Author.

Davies, J. (1996). *Educating students in a media-saturated culture.* Lancaster, PA: Technomic.

Dewey, J. (1938). *Experience and education.* New York: Macmillan.

Finders, K. (1992). Looking at lives through ethnography. *Educational Leadership, 50,* 60-65.

Freire, P. (1982). *Pedagogy of the oppressed.* New York: Continuum.

Gilligan, C. (1982). *In a different voice: Psychological theory and women's development.* Cambridge, MA: Harvard University Press.

Gilligan, C., Lyons, N., & Hanmer, T. (1990). *Making connections: The relational worlds of adolescent girls at Emma Willard School.* Cambridge: MA: Harvard University Press.

Gilligan, C., & Brown, L. M. (1992). *Meeting at the crossroads: The landmark book about the turning points in girls' and women's lives.* New York: Ballantine.

Goffman, E. (1979). *Gender advertisement.* Cambridge, MA: Harvard University Press.

Goodman, K., Bird, L. D., & Goodman, Y. M. (1991). *The whole language catalog.* Santa Rosa, CA: American School Publishers.

Havighurst, R. J. (1972). *Developmental tasks and education.* New York: David McKay & Co.

Heath, S.S. (1983). *Ways with words: Language, life, and work in communities and classrooms.* Cambridge, MA: Cambridge University Press.

Herbert, A. (1993). *Random acts of kindness*. Emeryville, CA: Conari Press.

Herbert, A. (1995). *Kids' Random Acts of Kindness*. Emeryville, CA: Conari Press.

Kohlberg, L. (1984). *The psychology of moral development: The nature and validity of moral stages, Vol. III.* San Francisco: Harper and Row.

Kohlberg, L. (1976). Moral stages and moralization: The cognitive-developmental approach. In T. Lickona (Ed.), *Moral development and behavior.* New York: Holt, Rinehart and Winston.

Lounsbury, J., & Vars, G. F. (1978). *A curriculum for the middle school years.* New York: Harper & Row.

Maanen, J. (1988). *Tales of the field: On writing ethnography.* Chicago: The University of Chicago Press.

Maslow, A. (1970). *Motivation and personality* (2nd ed.). New York: Harper & Row.

Ministry of Education. (1989). *Media literacy: Resource guide.* Ontario, Canada: Author.

National Middle School Association. (1995). *This we believe: Developmentally responsive middle level schools.* Columbus, OH: Author.

Oreinstein, P. (1994). *SchoolGirls, young women, self-esteem, and the confidence gap.* New York: Doubleday.

Piaget, J. (1952). *The origins of intelligence in children.* New York: International University Press.

Piper, M. (1994). *Reviving Ophelia: Saving the lives of adolescent girls.* New York; Ballantine Books.

Riley, L., Baldus, R., Belson, O., Schuler, B., & Keyes, M. (1993). *"My worst nightmare." Wisconsin students' perceptions of being the other gender.* Menomonie, WI: University Wisconsin-Stout.

Sadker, M., & Sadker, D. (1981). *Sex equity handbook for teachers.* New York: Longman.

Sadker, M., & Sadker, D. (1994). *Failing at fairness: How America's schools cheat girls.* New York: Charles Scribner's Son.

Stevenson, C. (1986). *Teachers as inquirers: Strategies for learning with and about early adolescents.* Columbus, OH: National Middle School Association.

Stevenson, C. (1992). *Teaching ten to fourteen year olds.* White Plains, NY: Longman Publishing Group.

Shuy, R. (1986). Language as a foundation for education: The school context. *Theory into practice* .{Special Issue}. 388-395.

Thomas, M. (1985). *Comparing theories of child development.* Belmont, CA: Wadsworth Publishing Company.

Appendix A

The statementaire distributed to students. Included are the oral comments the author made to assist students in responding to the questions.

––––––––

GRADE___AGE___MALE___FEMALE___SCHOOL_____
Number of sisters and brothers _____
Ages of brothers and sisters _____

American Indian, Alaska Native, or Aleut_____, Asian or Pacific Islander_____, White not of Hispanic origin_____, Hispanic origin_____, Black not of Hispanic origin_____

1. **Truth is...**
   If I ask you what truth is tell me your definition. For example, if you came home late and I ask you where you had been and said "now tell me the truth." Tell me the definition of truth you live by.

2. **Knowledge is...**
   You hear teachers talk about knowledge. What does knowledge mean to you?

3. **Power is...**
   Who has power? What kind of people or things?

4. **Who controls?**
   Who has control over things? What is control?

5. **Rules are...**
   What is your definition of rules? For example the Constitution provides a guideline of rules for the country. How do see rules of games, life, etc.?

6. **It is important to know...**
   What is important to know in order to get through life? For example a three-year-old would say your name and address. What would a 5th, 6th, 7th, or 8th grader say is important to know?

7. I would like to tell my friends...

If you could tell your friends something you have always wanted to tell them what would it be?

8. I would like to tell my family...

What would you like to tell your family? That you love them? Leave me alone? What do you think you would like to tell them that you don't feel comfortable telling them now?

9. I would like to advise my teachers...

Teachers are always giving you advice. What advice would you like to give them?

10. I would like to advise my principal...

What would you like to tell your principal?

11. I am happy when...

What makes you happy? When you are eating a pizza, or just bought something new?

12. A goal I have in life is to...

What is something you always wanted to do?

13. My favorite life experience is...

Of all the things you have done in your life, what is the absolute most favorite experience?

14. War is...

Now that the war is over, and you think or talk about it, what does war mean to you?

15. My favorite book is...

Of all the books you have read or had read to you which one do you like the most? Yes, comic books are OK.

16. My favorite movie is...

Of all the movies you have seen which one do you really like the best and that you would go see again, and again?

17. My three favorite TV shows are...

If you could watch any TV shows you wanted which ones

would you choose to watch?

18. **My favorite color is...**
What colors do you like to wear, fix your room up with?

19. **My favorite music is...**
What kind of music do you like to listen to when you have the opportunity?

20. **My two favorite songs are...**
Of all the music you like to listen to what are your two most favorite songs?

21. **My favorite sport to play is...**
When you have the opportunity to play any sport, what would you like to play?

22. **The best thing about my age...**
What is the neatest thing about your age? Tell me, what makes your age special.

23. **The worst thing about my age is...**
What is the worst thing about your age? Tell me, what makes being a _____ grader difficult.

24. **Another age I would like to be is ...**
Not that saying your age is good or bad but if you could be another age what would it be and why?

25. **What hasn't happened in your life you would like to happen...**
Would it be a college degree, visiting a certain place, owning something?

26. **I would like to tell the President of the U.S...**
If you could sit down for 15 minutes with the President what would you like to tell him?

27. **The most important invention since I've been born is...**
You have only been here for 10, 11, 12, 13, 14 years. What invention created in that time do you think is the most important? Examples might be microwave, video games, what else?

Most important invention ever...

Of all things that have ever been created, what is the most important to you?

28. **I feel bad when...**

   What makes you feel bad? When you forget to do something? Being teased?

29. **The last thing that made me feel bad was...**

   If you have felt bad what was the last thing that happened? Did you get teased recently, get hurt?

30. **I feel good when...**

   What makes you feel good, when you get your homework done, when you don't have a test?

   The last time I felt good was...

   What did someone say or do to make you feel good? Did someone smile at you today before school?

31. **To help myself feel better...**

   Not saying you ever feel bad, but if you do, what do you do to help yourself feel better? Take a walk? Scream? Listen to music? Throw pillows?

32. **If I could meet anyone living or dead, it would be _____because...**

   Of all the people in the world who would you like to meet and why? Albert Einstein, because he was so smart? Sally Ride because she is an astronaut?

33. **A friend is...**

   Most of us have friends. If I wanted to be your friend what qualities would you want me to have?

34. **A best friend is...**

   What qualities would I need if I wanted to be your best friend? Tell me the difference between being your friend and being your best friend.

35. The best thing about my gender is...

What is the neatest thing about being a girl? About being a boy?

36. The worst thing about my gender is...

What's not so great about being a boy or a girl? Are there any problems?

37. The biggest differences between the sexes is...

Other than body parts, what are things that make men and women different?

38. In my free time I like to...

When you have nothing to do, no homework, no chores, what do you like to do? Take a walk? Go to a movie?

39. My favorite joke is...

What makes you laugh? What kind of jokes do you tell each other? Yes, you can write a dirty joke.

40. My favorite food is...

If I were to have a party for _____ graders what kind of food would I have to have to make the party a success?

41. When I think of the future I...

When you think of the future what do you think you think about? Describe what life might be.

42. I worry about...

I hope you don't worry. But if you do worry, what concerns you? What you will have for dinner? What the world will be like when you get older?

43. Language is...

When you hear the word 'language' what do you think about? A class? Another country? What people say?

44. A good teacher is...

What are the qualities that you like in a good teacher? Someone who helps you?

45. A good student is...

Teachers have their definition of a good student, what do you students think make a good student? Answers a lot of questions?

46. A good principal is...

When you think of your principal, or principals in general, what qualities make a good principal?

47. My career goal is to...

Ten to fifteen years from now what do you see yourself doing? Be a pilot? astronaut? teacher? What are you going to do to pay your bills?

48. My favorite subject is...

Of all the classes you take and the subjects you study, which ones do you like to go to and study?

49. My least favorite subject is...

Of all the classes you go to or study, which ones do you like going to least of all?

50. What I like best about school is...

What do you like about going to school? Describe what makes school worth coming to.

51. What I like least about schools is...

What don't you like about coming to school? Describe what makes school not fun to come to?

52. My role model is...

Who is someone you would like to be like? Describe their qualities.

53. Is there something I should have asked that I didn't?

I know I have asked you to think about a lot of things, but is there anything I missed? Anything you would like to ask other kids? If you have a question write it down, and if you want to answer go ahead and respond if you want to.

Appendix B

Selected questions with a sampling of responses by grade level and gender.

————————

4. Who controls?

Grade 5

Girls	Boys
My parents and God.	I control
Teacher, parents, older people.	The government
Something that people do	Parents
to be safe	You control yourself
Jesus	Brain
President, my parents.	Adults
God or government.	
Mom.	

Grade 6

God	Adults
Laws	God
Presidents	Presidents
Parents	Sometimes it's one person
Someone who tells you to do stuff	and sometimes another
I control my life	person
Government	Family
Laws, presidents,	Parents
police, parents	Parents
and God	Middle-age people
"Me," parents, and principal	You control yourself

Grade 7

President, adults	Power or money, people with
Parents, President, and babysitter	money
if you have one	God
Money and the government	The people
Well-liked people, the rich	Money, adults, teachers
or famous	Elders
The elite class	Older peope
God	Society
The oldest person in the group	The atom bomb
My parents, teachers and staff	
of my school, otherwise me	

Grade 8

Mom
God
Adults
Myself
Parents, adults
Government
Money
You have control over yourself
The person in charge

Money, God, parents
Parents
I do
Government
Adults
Me
Whoever is in charge
Person with the most power

---

6. It is important to know...

Grade 5

Girls

Subjects we are talking about.
Peoples' addresses for
an emergency.
To stay away from drugs.
Your homework assignments.
History, math, and reading.
Your work and your address.
The truth.
Not to do drugs.
How to stay alive.

Boys

An education
School
Math, language
You're not perfect
Not to do drugs
Your address
That I am a good friend
The dress code
What your decision is.
What's going on in the world

Grade 6

Respect
School
How to learn
Who you are inside
How to get good grades
Not to take drugs and all the
stuff you learn in school
To go on with life
If your parents love you

What the rules are
What's right and what's
wrong
Yourself and feelings
How far you can go before
you get into trouble
Friends and some teachers
How to act around people

APPENDIX B

Life
Yourself
What's going on in the world
Your rights
Instructions, how to get out of
trouble, to practice, to do
something good or bad
How to take care of yourself

About girls
About you
Who your friends are
Your subjects
Math, reading
The basics
How to use time wisely
How to get along with others

Grade 7

About life (teachers and grades)
How to say no
Math & science really well
Foreign language,
Reading
The latest fashions, who's going with
whom, friends phone numbers,
having friends
Who you are and want to become
The truth and your surroundings
Manners
How to handle money and to be able
to drive yourself
Where you plan on going in life
How to say no
That your parents will always be there

Academics, math, reading,
speaking
How to say no and
who your friends are
Who you friends are
Who you are
What you are going to do
with your life
Phone numbers, CPR and
how to avoid a fire, etc. in
case of an semergency
What class is next
As much as you possibly can
Your name
Knowledge
What is right and wrong

Grade 8

Who to trust
Who your friends are
Reading
Your social security number
How to read and write
Your necessities
How your friends think about you
About life
How other people act in different
situations
What you are learning in school
Right from wrong
What's good and bad, and what you
think
When to say no
About the heart
Not to get pregnant at a young age
How to survive, get along with other
people, have an education

About life, education
Who your friends are
Each other
How to get along with others
Right from wrong
Rules in school
How to live
How to change the grade on
your report card
School subjects
Your age
Read and write
To be a Christian
That money equals power
How to do things

APPENDIX B

That you are loved and that
someday your mother will
understand you
All about drugs, sex, and
peer pressure, know all you are
gett §ing into
What is going on around you,
like current affairs

———

8. I would like to tell my family...

Grade 5

Girls

To pay more attention to me
How I feel
To stop bossing me just becaue
I am the youngest
Not to hit me
When something happens
at school
Everything about school
Stop treating me like a baby
Let me have more friends
over
Let's move to another town
Let's get rich
Stay out of my bedroom
To let me have my own phone
To give me some privacy

Boys

To let me do what I want to
do
About school
Don't blame me for stuff
my sister does
I'm lazy, so don't bug me
I would do many things
for them
To work together
I'm having trouble with
math
It's not easy
Secrets
I am doing well in school
No matter where you are or
what you do I love you

Grade 6

I love them very much
Thanks
What I am doing in school
A lot
I don't know what to do with
myself
We need to do more things
together
All kinds of things
I don't want to move
Leave me alone

I love you
Nothing
Stay clean about things
Get me a new bike
Who I like
Don't ground me all the
time
They are nice to me
Move away
Yelling doesn't teach a lesson
They are the best

APPENDIX B

How I am doing in school
and how kids treat me
You are special
Lighten up/respect us more
They helped me through the years
Bug off
Stay out of my life

To have my own privacy
Not so much work
To get rich
Stay out of private life
When I do bad on a test
Don't be so strict/let me do
more things without asking
permission

Grade 7

Leave me alone.
I love them.
What I feel
I love them
The truth
For my sister to give me more
privacy
That I am a unique individual
Important things, events, how I am
doing in school
That I am not really happy the
way I am

To understand me
I love them
I love them, ease up,
be more fun
Nothing
To quit fighting
Life is boring
That lots of things they
aren't in good judgment
The things I feel, but they
wouldn't understand

Grade 8

Thank you
Everything/thanks for being there
I love them
Be easy on us
Be nicer to me
When I have problems or questions
If I get a good grade
I love them, even though I'm crabby
and I yell at them, it's not towards
them
I am moving out
To be closer
How nice mom's been
Not to scream
That I exist too
When I have problems or questions
I go to a friend's house on Thursday
That I'm insecure, very insecure
They should loosen their grip on me
I need to grow up some way or the other
To quit being possessive and over protective

That I love them
How I feel
That I can do a lot of stuff
on my own
The truth
Leave me alone
Let me do more things
To leave me alone when I
want to be left alone
Stay healthy
To raise my allowance
Stuff that would get them
mad and get me in trouble
Quiet

11. I am happy when...

Grade 5

Girls

People make me feel good.
Having fun.
No homework.
When friends like me.
When my parents laugh.
When with girlfriend
When I get good grades.
When something good happens to me.
I am with my relatives.
My birthday.
My cat doesn't bite me.
When I do a good deed or on vaation.
My parents do something nice for me.
People do what I want.

Boys

When I accomplished a good deed.
When I get something I want
I win
I get good grades
People treat me nicely
It's my birthday
I get A's
I am playing sports
I accomplish something
I have money
When we eat good or buy clothes
When we go eat pizza
When I have friends

Grade 6

My family is together and gets pizza
I'm with my best friends and when we're having a good education
Go on vacation
When school is out
I'm with family and friends
Teachers and parents leave me alone and when I get good grades
When I just feel happy
When I get to go somewhere
I'm with my friends, get good grades, or seeing my family
I go out

Pass a test
I travel
I'm playing sports with my friends
Someone who I like, likes me
I fool around
I accomplish something
Play Nintendo and role-playing games
When I get money
I am around friends
Things go right
I get a new toy
I can take it easy
We win a baseball game
When I can do something by myself

Grade 7

Somebody says something nice
I don't have homework
It makes me feel important
I am happy when family and friends listen to what I have to say.

I know I've done well on something and when I am with my friends
I have money
I play sports and talk on the phone

APPENDIX B

I go shopping or just have a one on
one talk with a friend
I get what I want and learning more
I'm talking on the phone, shopping,
or when I win a race
With my friends and family
I'm with my friends and having
a lot of fun

I am around my friends
Something new
I am having an adventurous
time
I am with friends
School's out
I have sex
When certain teachers are
absent
I am passing classes

Grade 8

I am with friends
I get good grades
Everything is great
When I am not sick
The people around me are happy
My family gets along
Sleeping
Someone does something nice to me
A guy I like, likes me
I'm having fun with my friends and
when I get good grades
Playing Nintendo
When the people around me are happy
I accomplish my goals
Get new clothes, new sneakers, my
birthday
Mom doesn't tell me what to do
I have time for myself, and don't have
anything to worry about

I succeed in life
I get money and good grades
I am with my friends
Playing sports
My parents don't bother me
Things go my way
I am by myself
I have a free study hall
I use my computer
Something good happens to
me
I go to my friend's house
Things go right

————

22. The best thing about my age...

Grade 5

Girls	Boys
I don't know	I don't get much homework
That I am growing up	Able to do more
Going to school	Things to help my mom
I can do more things	More privileges
Privileges	I get to go on big rides
Now I can go out for sports	I'm older than most 5th
Still a kid	graders
Being the oldest	Get to do more things
Sports	I can still ride my bike
Parents treat you more mature	Freedom/Stay out longer

Grade 6

I still have a longer life
I'm just beginning to be a teen
Nothing
Is sometimes getting a lot of
attention
I like to play and be with my friends
I can have fun
Parents can trust you on your own
I can do a lot
Nothing, I hate it
I get to do more things than I used to
Having many friends
Being adventurous
I can go out for sports and be the right
height for rides
Almost grown up
Lots of friends
I am younger than all my friends
I am going to be a teenager and can
do anything I want.
I can act like a kid but also like
an adult.
Old enough to go more places by myself

Nothing special, but I get
more privileges
I'm half way through school
I'm young
I can't get arrested
Can work for my parents
You can be yourself
I don't have as many
responsibilities
Go almost anyway
Older than 5th graders
Being a kid
I am a teenager
I get to ride my bike to town
I can do fun activities
Responsibility
Nothing
That I am older than my
brothers do things they
can't
Know much more about life
I can do a lot of bad stuff
Not in elementary school
Getting older/Staying out
later

Grade 7

Getting new clothes because you're
grown up
It's okay to ask anything and learning
about things
Knowing I have a long life ahead of me
Is enjoying to be young while I can
Get to meet more guys.
Getting to do things with my friends
without my parents being there
Can do things or a kid or act as an adult
More freedom
I get to participate in more things
I get to do more things alone
Adult menus in a restaurant
I'm one of the youngest and I can still
get in places for free
You get trusted and to baby sit

Going through so many
changes
Because they think I'm
under 10
I am sill young
That I get to watch PG-13
movies
I can do more things and be
trusted more
I can see PG-13 and ride
most roller coasters
I can be really active
I am becoming an adult
Being a teenager
I am almost in high school
Being older than my
brothers
I'm old

Grade 8

I get to participate in more activities	Freedom
There is no good thing	More money
Get to do more, more freedom	Get to do more things
Boys	That I can succeed in a lot
Friends	of things
My life's ahead of me	More privileges
I'm not too old	Going to high school next
Two more years until I drive	year
Get to be with your friends	You start to look better
Being a teenager, we finally start to	I am a middle age boy
understand things	I get to graduate from this
Get to experience life a little	crappy school
Next year I'll be in high school	I am staring to get to do
Don't have to worry about bills	what I want
or gas money	I can get away with a lot of
All the activities I can be in	stuff
Oldest in the school	Getting more power
Go lots of places	More privileges, more
Not always treated like a child	money, more obligations
Parents trust us more	Staying up later
I have a lot of friends	Nothing
Can get into a PG-13 movie	Do more stuff
without a parent	I can't go to jail
I'm trusted more and listened to more	Being a teenager
by grownups.	I'm young and can do a lot
	of things

---

23. The worst thing about my age...

Grade 5

Girls	Boys
Growing up	Being the youngest and
Being caught between being a	getting beat up
little kid and a teenager	School
Getting blamed all the time	People make fun of us
I am not old enough to drive	It's some place between 0-
Parents	20
Too much homework	Can't drive/have a car get
Not going on trips with dad.	into clubs
Having to go to school	More responsibilities
I can't go to the mall with my friends	Being able to do things my
Classes are harder.	brother can
I am the youngest in my family	Chores

Grade 6

Not being able to do everything yet
Not old enough
I'm ignored
Getting put down because of my age
People treat you like a baby and don't really understand you
Can't drive
Curfew in town, can't go on trips by myself
Nothing/I hate it
Can't go to R rated movies
Maturing/going through puberty
Putting up with parents' stupid rules
Too tall
I get made fun of. I was held back and people know I am older and make fun of me
Can't go anywhere without my parent
Can't go out with my friends
Have to follow rules
I can have a baby

I still have a long time in school
Responsibility
I am not a teenager yet
Not having enough freedom
A lot of pressure
Parents
Littler than eighth graders
Can't drive
I can't make any decisions
Terrible years
Nothing
Babysitting my sister
Can't do what I want
I am the oldest and get blamed for everything
Growing older
I am too young
My height
I have to do more chores
People still think I am a kid

Grade 7

Too much time before I get my license
Not being paid attention to
Liked one day and dumped the next
I'm getting older
School
Most people (family, adults) don't take us seriously
A lot of homework in school
I'm too far away from my parents
Having to babysit my younger brothers and sisters
Too young to do things on my own
I'm younger and look younger
I'm still not a teenager
I'm still not a teenager
It's harder, everyone treats you different.

I have to go to school
Working
I am too young to do a lot of things
Drive
I change too much
Everything
I can't go into those fun play pens (too tall)
I'm young/I'm too tall
People think 13-year-olds are supposed to be bad
All the changes
All the relatives try to embrace me
Not old enough to do anything

Grade 8

More responsibilities
Not enough freedom, too young
Puberty/period
Too young
Everyone has mood changes and gets into fights sometimes.
Not treated as an adult
Friends complaining about own looks and lots of pressure to look like Cindy Crawford
I still have to live with my parents
To get a lot of homework
Older siblings made mistakes so can't do things they did
Peer Pressure
Parents expect too much
Too many chores
Don't understand everything
Parents don't trust us as much.
Usually treated like a child, people don't realize how much we have grown up and the pressure we have.
People don't truly think 14-years- old do drugs, drink, and have sex

I get blamed for everything
Too young
My parents have too many limits
Younger than my older siblings
School
Everyone hates us
Computer companies don't take me seriously
Can't drive
My parents worry about me too much
Not enough money
Having an older brother
Everything
Brothers fight with me
I don't have as much freedom as I want
Being the oldest
Parents, drugs, people

———

35. The best thing about my gender is...

Grade 5

Girls	Boys
Hair	Not being a girl
More clothes advantages	Able to play pro sports
I can look sexy	We get to play sports
I don't know	Stand up to pee
Being pretty	Don't have to have a baby
Make-up	We're stronger
I don't have to fix dirty things	I don't know
Able to have children	I'm a man
Sit down to go toilet	I can be in the Air Force
Being able to have a child	We get the better locker room
Grow faster than boys	No girls in certain clubs
You don't have to go to war	I don't have to wear dresses

Grade 6

Hair
You can shop a lot
Being delicate
Boys treat us better
You don't always have to do something
like farm work
Sometimes having attention
You get nice clothes
I don't know
Nothing
I am prettier than boys
Being pretty and flexible
Women are better than men
It is good and great

Not being a girl
Don't have to have babies
We're better than girls
We're smarter
Sports
Known for being just a tad
bit better than girls
Lots of hair
I am stronger
I play sports better
I'm a man
Don't have to worry about
getting pregnant or using
tampons
Most men explore more
things

Grade 7

I look pretty
Not having to do hard chores
Men treat us well & always think of us
first
We can do things males can't
Being able to have a family
We have long hair.
The magic of having children
I'm able to give life
Get to meet guys
We like to shop
Don't have to pay for things on dates.
Wearing cute clothes, long hair
shopping, ears pierced.
Don't have to fight anyone and
then be called a wimp

It is the best
Stronger
Have more opportunities
Boys rule
That boys take things easier
Boys always have to make
the moves
Don't have to have a baby
I get to do more of the work
We do certain things girls
can't and are generally more
active
Nothing
We tend to have more stress
Males are expected to do
more work
Don't have to wear a dress
Get to do things girls can't
I'm rough

Grade 8

We can wear anything
Liking boys
We get to look pretty
We can't get in many fights
Nobody is like you

Not being a girl
Sports ability
Stronger
Can play football
I like being a boy

APPENDIX B

We can't get drafted
We get to meet cute guys
Nothing
I don't know
Having babies.
We don't have to go to war
Having *Seventeen* and *YM* to help us
live our daily lives, the women's
movement, and defending ourselves
by telling guys to get a life
I can be smart
Looking at boys
We're noticeable
and provocative
Going shopping all the time and
you don't have to do hard things
like boys
We can experience the birth of a baby
have long nails, long hair, wear
dresses, skirts, shirts, and pants

We have more opportunities
in the world
We can go out and get real
dirty
We have to be rude
No PMS
Don't have to give birth to
babies
We get to watch girls
Professional sports
Males are stronger
Strength
Nice to have bikes, skate
boards, wheelers
You can't get pregnant
Able to do more things
Making girls get pregnant,
,

---

35. The worst thing about my gender is...

Grade 5

Girls	Boys
It takes forever to do my hair	Nothing
I have to clean house	I don't know
Going through physical pain	Can't wear dresses
I have to do dishes	Having to wear tight clothes
Having to deal with sexist males	We have to stick up for girls
Being lady like	I have to go last
Not getting equal rights as men	We do all the work
Having to wear dresses and pantyhose	Not being able to sew
I can't be in pro sports	
Can't do things that boys do	
People think I am not as good as boys	

Grade 6

Periods	Nothing, it's awesome
We have to do things like clean	Don't know.
Boys don't have kids	I have blond hair
You can't have everything	I can't hit girls
Sometimes not getting any attention	My odor.

APPENDIX B

Having other girls snob you
Boys don't think that girls can play
baseball and soccer
Not as athletic
Boys are jerks and are sexist
Prejudice
Puberty
Nothing, I like being this sex
Messed up skin
I have to take a shower in 7th grade
So many different clothes to choose from
Get more diseases from sex
We feel more about feelings
Having to worry about your period
in school.

Growing old as a male
We are always at fault
Different thoughts
Puberty comes slow
Clothes
I have to do hard work
I don't get in on gossip

Grade 7

Adolescence
Traditional stereotypes.
Don't have the same or as many

trary to surveys
We have periods
Takes too long to get ready
Having to have babies/birth
That boys think they are so much
better
Not considered as good as boys
Guys get to do more things
Getting treated unequally
The way the male ego gets to me
Can't be on major league teams
Most people think we are too sensitive

Nothing
Can't think of anything
Teachers favor girls, con-
opportunities as male

Less caring
Don't know
We have more stress
Males are expected to do
more work
We do the yard work
The girls are forward
I am worked harder at home
People blame us for stuff
We usually die earlier

Grade 8

Pregnancy
Babies
Guys tend to take advantage
PMS
You get treated unequally
Growing-up
My period
Curfews
We get smacked around more
People don't take you seriously
People make a big deal if females can
play sports or do what guys do

Nothing
We get discriminated
against at school
There isn't one
I am not real strong
I don't know
Pressure
It hurts to get kicked
in the ____
Want to have fun with each
other
Fat

APPENDIX B

Assumption girls are late because of
hair,make-up, etc.
Expected to be more responsible
Never be able to get as good as job as men
People are sexist and think women can't
succeed in life
Not enough opportunities
The stereotype that men are better
than women
Can't take off your shirt when you get hot
There are a lot of dirty jokes about women

————

42. I worry about...

Grade 5

Girls	Boys
A lot of things, growing up	School
Getting bad grades	Pollution
School and homework	Talk
Getting into my 50s	Family Stuff
My family	My parents/brothers/sisters
Drugs	My health
My parents may die	My health
Wars	My girlfriend dumping me
My family, everything	Things that are supposed to
Boys	be done in the future
Being poor	Unsafe sex.
Having a bad sickness	If soldiers come home safely
Myself	Death and war
About the environment	The earth
Dying	Death
Animal Extinction	My bladder exploding
Getting in trouble	

Grade 6

Death/crime	Grades
Life	Dying
Doing something wrong	My future
Nothing	What the world will be like
My sister	Drugs
My parents dying	My whole family
If I have a problem when I babysit	AIDS
My mom dying	What's going to happen

My future
My big brother
If I am going to be who I think
I'm going to be
Having my period in school
Getting pregnant
The world exploding
My family and the earth
Boys
My family and me
How the world will be in 2000
My sisters getting hurt or dying
How some of my friends will turn out

Nothing
Games and friends
Being killed or kidnapped
How I am going to turn out
Dying, getting murdered
My mom
The ozone layer in outer
space
World War III
Girls
Violence
Getting in trouble for
something
Pollution

Grade 7

My brothers/sisters/parents
My looks and my popularity level and
my grades
Getting into fights and not being friends
anymore
The world ending, environment
High school, worry about the pressures:
peer, pressure in athletics
pressure to succeed academically
Getting a deadly disease
Grades, family deaths
Fires, they ruin my things
The future
The situation the environment is in
Who will win the election
The world ending
How I will turn out and if the world will
be there
Death/war/being in earthquakes
Life, love, and the end of school
Losing my family
How I look, if I am ugly, too thin for
my nose

Being poor
My mother's job
How I look
I don't have a worry
Being shot or killed
Parents
Life
Competition
The world
That I am going to do good
in life
My grandpa and I hope the
world doesn't get too
modernized
Breaking my neck
Leaving my family
Dying
Parents dying
Schoolwork
Grades

Grade 8

How good or bad I did on a test
If my parents will ever get a divorce
My grades, my hair
School
Won't be good enough
What people think of me, do they
like me, do they not like me, why,
why not?

Girls
Dying
Nothing
People getting older
People
My homework getting done
Losing power

APPENDIX B

Bad grades, doing bad
My appearance
Grades, appearance, weight
Too much, graduating
Money
My parents dying
Being homeless
Dying
Bills
Life/the earth/people/war
Family, my brothers and sisters
Failure
The future
Whispering of a friend or people
in the class that are talking about me
Being killed for a coat, racial situations,
or someone will kill Clinton (I like him),
Friends will die of AIDS.

Demerits
World War III
The earth
Grades
The year 2000, whether we
will be or not
My family
My dog
My stupid life
The world

———

44. A good teacher is...

Grade 5

Girls	Boys
A fun one that makes learning fun	Nice
Is kind and doesn't give a lot	Humorous
of homework	A person who teaches well
Help students	and does give homework
Doesn't yell	Teaches you knowledge
Not mean	Cares
Caring	One who doesn't yell
Understanding	Explains everything
Spends time/helps their students	Teaches you something
Doesn't give lots of test	
Fun and nice, but strict some of the time	
Respects you	
A nice attitude	

Grade 6

Kind, understanding, but still teaches you.	Nice
There is none	Makes things funny
Likes everyone	Who understands
Teaches well	One that makes us learn
	Doesn't give homework

Brings out funny things
and happiness in learning
makes kids want to learn
Understanding
Listens to questions and concerns
 Doesn't yell and give a lot of homework
Teaches well, but goofs off
once in awhile

Nice and has fun but
teaches students well
Is easy going and is fun
Helps and doesn't criticize
How much time you put in
and patient

Grade 7

Cares about kids, likes and helps kids
giver
Discusses with you, does fun things
in class, and helps if in need
Makes school exciting and cares
Understanding, thoughtful considerate,
nice.
Patient, understanding, nice, firm,
doesn't criticize
Nice, caring, funny, sensitive
Gives homework
Has fun, is a kid at heart, does not
 blabber on about different subjects

Fun, caring, homework

Nice, fair, and fun, no
homework
Tells jokes
Nice, caring, and moves her
students
Makes learning fun, by
doing things
A good sense of humor
Nice
Makes learning fun

Grade 8

Cares
Someone who gets the points across
Someone who gives homework
Teach by having fun at the same time
Helpful/One you can trust
Someone who is not a one-way thinker
Sympathetic
Someone who doesn't pick on people
A fun teacher
Who doesn't hold things against you.
Doesn't have favorites
Interesting
Keeps class under control,
teaches good

Somebody who understands
my needs
One who teaches good and
gives no homework
Makes you laugh
Having fun
When they help you
Smart
A teacher who spills out
everything she knows
No teacher/There aren't any
Intelligent
Someone who is cool
A fun teacher, nice home
work

APPENDIX B

Voice comes from a deeper place than our throats. Voice comes from our heart, from our minds, and from the deepest places of knowing and feeling.

— Penny Oldfather, 1993

NATIONAL MIDDLE SCHOOL ASSOCIATION

National Middle School Association was established in 1973 to serve as a voice for professionals and others interested in the education of young adolescents. The Association has grown rapidly and now enrolls members in all fifty states, the Canadian provinces, and forty-two other nations. In addition, fifty-three state, regional, and provincial middle school associations are official affiliates of NMSA.

NMSA is the only association dedicated exclusively to the education, development, and growth of young adolescents. Membership is open to all. While middle level teachers and administrators make up the bulk of the membership, central office personnel, college and university faculty, state department officials, other professionals, parents, and lay citizens are also actively involved in supporting our single mission – improving the educational experiences of 10-15 year olds. This open and diverse membership is a particular strength of NMSA.

The Association provides a variety of services, conferences, and materials in fulfilling its mission. In addition to *Middle School Journal*, the movement's premier professional journal, the Association publishes *Research in Middle Level Education Quarterly*, a wealth of books and monographs, videos, an association newsletter, a magazine, and occasional papers. The Association's highly acclaimed annual conference, which has drawn over 10,000 registrants in recent years, is held in the fall.

For information about NMSA and its many services contact the Headquarters at 2600 Corporate Exchange Drive, Suite 370, Columbus, Ohio 43231, TELEPHONE 800-528-NMSA, FAX 614-895-4750.

NMSA

For more information about NMSA, detach and mail the card below – no postage necessary. If you want to call use our toll free number 800-528-NMSA

Yes, I would like the following information: **1242**

____ Catalog of publications and resources
____ List of upcoming conferences and workshops
____ Membership details and classifications
____ Subscription to *Middle School Journal*
____ Subscription to *Research in Middle Level Education Quarterly*

NAME _____

MAILING ADDRESS_____

_____

                                                            1242

Yes, I would like the following information:

____ Catalog of publications and resources
____ List of upcoming conferences and workshops
____ Membership details and classifications
____ Subscription to *Middle School Journal*
____ Subscription to *Research in Middle Level Education Quarterly*

NAME _____

MAILING ADDRESS _____

_____

BUSINESS REPLY MAIL

First Class Mail   Permit No. 3356 Columbus, OH

POSTAGE WILL BE PAID BY ADDRESSEE

NATIONAL MIDDLE SCHOOL ASSOCIATION

2600 CORPORATE EXCHANGE DRIVE STE 370

COLUMBUS OH 43231-9992

BUSINESS REPLY MAIL

First Class Mail   Permit No. 3356 Columbus, OH

POSTAGE WILL BE PAID BY ADDRESSEE

NATIONAL MIDDLE SCHOOL ASSOCIATION

2600 CORPORATE EXCHANGE DRIVE STE 370

COLUMBUS OH 43231-9992

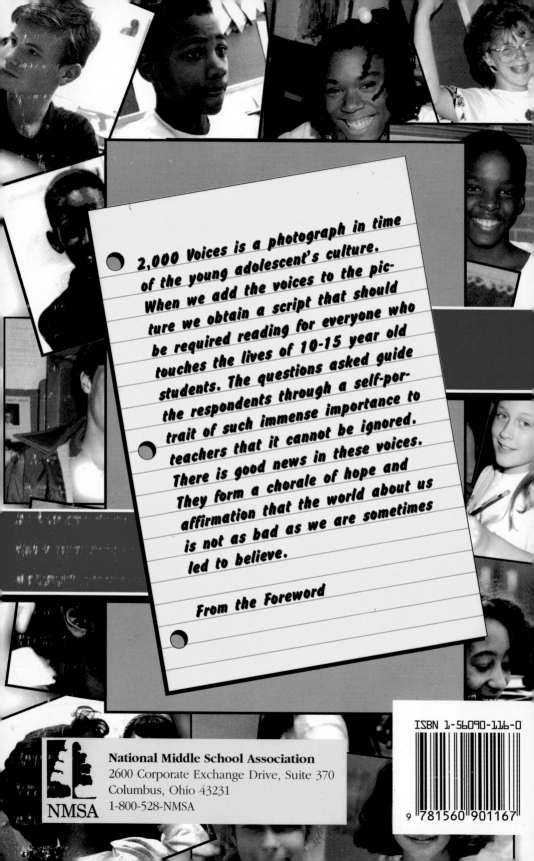

2,000 Voices is a photograph in time of the young adolescent's culture. When we add the voices to the picture we obtain a script that should be required reading for everyone who touches the lives of 10-15 year old students. The questions asked guide the respondents through a self-portrait of such immense importance to teachers that it cannot be ignored. There is good news in these voices. They form a chorale of hope and affirmation that the world about us is not as bad as we are sometimes led to believe.

From the Foreword

ISBN 1-56090-116-0

National Middle School Association
2600 Corporate Exchange Drive, Suite 370
Columbus, Ohio 43231
1-800-528-NMSA

NMSA

9 781560 901167